The Other Side of Pain

Darkness to Dawn:

From Hurt to Healing to Hope

Dr. Shumonte Cooper

ISBN: 979-8-9878940-8-8

Printed in the United States of America

Table of Contents

The Genius of Pain - *Pain Level 4*: A mild discomfort, much like the first instances of scraped knees or bruised elbows in childhood. The pain is noticeable but easily brushed aside.

A Soldier's Stride - *Pain Level 8*: The intensity of military combat, both mentally and physically, brings the pain close to its peak. It's sharp, consistent, and almost unbearable.

Fractured Familiarity - *Pain Level 9*: The pain is sharp as in combat, the persistent ache of feeling out of place, surrounded by what should be familiar.

Muted Celebrations - *Pain Level 8*: A heavy heart, a mix of sadness and longing.

Scars of Service - *Pain Level 10*: One of the most excruciating phases, where hopelessness engulfs, and the emotional pain feels almost tangible. Mostly unbearable days and nights.

Faith's Flourish - *Pain Level 9*: Though there's a glimmer of hope and connection, there's still a significant pain in rediscovering oneself, akin to the sensation of an old wound being stretched.

"In the mirror of time, we see the echoes of who we were and the shadows of who we may yet become." ~Anonymous

Preface

Each of us carries within our souls a tapestry of emotions and memories. At times, this tapestry feels woven with threads of joy, while at other moments, it bears the heavy stitches of pain. It's easy to share stories of happiness and triumph, yet often, our tales of hurt and despair remain hidden, buried deep within, shadowed by shame or fear. Pain has a unique way of introducing us to our strongest selves, threading through our lives and leaving its imprint on every chapter. It was the elusive constant in my life, always present, always shaping—though not always understood.

I felt compelled to pen this narrative not for accolades or empathy but because I recognize that countless souls grapple daily with pain—pain that spans various facets of existence. Some wounds are visible, while others lurk silently beneath the surface. Each one, however, leaves an indelible mark on our spirit.

Through the chapters of my life, I've navigated treacherous terrains of hurt, from the childhood aches of rejection to the intense traumas of adulthood. Yet, as you'll soon discover, my journey didn't end in desolation. Instead, the path meandered toward healing, understanding, and eventual peace.

Born into a world punctuated by pain, I was eventually reborn into a realm of serenity and strength. My transformation wasn't instantaneous or easy. It took years of introspection, guidance, and relentless determination to find light amidst the shadows.

It is my hope that by sharing my personal odyssey—from pain to peace—you, dear reader, will find solace, inspiration, and perhaps a mirror to your own experiences. If my testament helps even one individual inch closer to the other side of pain, every word penned here will have served its purpose.

The journey might be long, and the road might be rough, but on the other side of the pain lies a tranquility so profound that it's worth every step. So, with an open heart and a spirit of vulnerability, I welcome you to journey with me through some of the pages of my life, exploring, understanding, and ultimately finding solace in knowing that even amidst the depths of pain, there lies the other side—a sanctuary where peace resides.

THE NATURES OF PAIN

Physical and Emotional

Physical Pain: At its core, physical pain acts as a body's alarm system. It's a signal that something is wrong. From a scraped knee in childhood to the deeper wounds sustained in adulthood or the battlefield, physical pain is a constant reminder of our vulnerabilities. The immediate sensation can range from a dull ache to an overwhelming, sharp agony. But even after the physical wounds heal, they often leave behind scars, which can be lasting reminders of past traumas.

Emotional Pain: Often intertwined with physical pain, emotional pain can sometimes be even more debilitating. It stems from a myriad of sources:

Childhood Challenges

Rejection: From being picked last in a schoolyard game to feeling neglected or misunderstood by parents or guardians, the pain of rejection can seed insecurities that persist into adulthood. This early feeling of "not being enough" can manifest in various ways, influencing behaviors and choices.

People Pleasing: A coping mechanism that many adopt to counteract feelings of rejection. The child who was once overlooked or undervalued might grow into an adult constantly seeking validation, often at the expense of their own well-being or desires.

Adulthood Challenges

War: The horrors of war inflict both physical and emotional scars. Soldiers and civilians alike may face traumas that linger long after conflicts end. The loss of comrades, exposure to violence, and the sheer weight of survival can lead to profound emotional disturbances, such as PTSD.

Broken Promises: Trust, once shattered, can be difficult to mend. Betrayals, whether in personal relationships or professional settings, can result in deep-seated feelings of mistrust and wariness.

The Lingering Effects

The accumulation of these pains often leads to emotional baggage. This can manifest in myriad ways: anxiety, depression, trust issues, or even physical symptoms triggered by emotional distress. The constant pursuit of external validation, lingering traumas from war, or the hesitance to trust again after betrayal are all manifestations of the past pains echoing into the present.

Understanding the nature of pain, both physical and emotional, is crucial. Recognizing its sources and manifestations can pave the way for healing. Just as a wound needs tending to heal properly, emotional and psychological wounds require attention, care, and often professional guidance.

1. Biological Link:

Neurotransmitters: Both pain and depression are associated with neurotransmitters like serotonin and norepinephrine. Changes in the levels of these neurotransmitters can affect mood and pain perception.

Brain Structures: Areas of the brain like the amygdala, prefrontal cortex, and the anterior cingulate cortex play roles in mood regulation and pain perception. Alterations or imbalances in these areas can contribute to both depression and heightened pain sensitivity.

2. Pain Leading to Depression:

Chronic Pain: Individuals suffering from chronic pain conditions (e.g., fibromyalgia, arthritis, migraines) often develop depressive symptoms over time. The persistent nature of their pain can limit their activities, lead to isolation, and diminish their overall quality of life.

Loss of Function: Pain might limit an individual's ability to work, engage in social activities, or even perform daily tasks. This loss of function can lead to feelings of worthlessness or despair.

Sleep Disruption: Chronic pain often disrupts sleep patterns. Over time, sleep deprivation can contribute to depressive symptoms.

3. Depression Amplifying Pain:

Perception of Pain: Those with depression often perceive pain more acutely. Their lowered mood and decreased cognitive function can amplify the pain's intensity and make it harder to manage.

Decreased Coping: Depression can diminish an individual's ability to cope with pain, making them more susceptible to feelings of hopelessness and exacerbating the cycle of pain and depression.

Physical Inactivity: Depression can lead to fatigue and a lack of motivation to be active. Physical inactivity can worsen certain types of pain, especially musculoskeletal pain.

4. Shared Risk Factors:

Both pain and depression can result from shared predisposing factors, including genetic predisposition, past trauma or injury, or chronic medical conditions.

5. Treatment Challenges:

Complex Management: Treating an individual with both pain and depression can be challenging due to the overlapping symptoms and the potential for certain treatments to affect both conditions.

Medication Interactions: Some medications for depression can help alleviate pain, while others might not be effective or could even exacerbate pain.

Therapeutic Interventions: Cognitive-behavioral therapy (CBT) has shown effectiveness in treating both depression and pain, as it addresses the interrelated cognitive, behavioral, and emotional facets of both conditions.

6. Benefit of Integrated Treatment:

Recognizing the relationship between pain and depression underscores the importance of an integrated treatment approach. Addressing both conditions simultaneously often yields better outcomes than treating them separately.

Pain and depression have a bidirectional relationship where one can trigger or worsen the other. Understanding this connection is crucial for effective diagnosis and treatment. These are all the areas my therapists have covered over the years with me. The key takeaway is you must still do the work to recover even after the diagnosis.

If someone suspects they are experiencing both, seeking professional medical and psychological assistance is essential.

UNDERSTANDING PAIN: A BRIEF SYNOPSIS

Before delving into "The Other Side of Pain," it's essential to understand the enigma of pain. What, exactly, is pain? At its core, pain is a complex experience intertwined with our physical, emotional, and even societal fabric.

Most medical professionals utilize a scale ranging from 1 to 10 to gauge the intensity of pain. But what do these numbers signify? A '1' might denote a minor annoyance, a slight discomfort, while a '10' represents an unbearable agony, the kind that can make someone wish for an end to it all.

However, these numbers aren't absolute. They're subjective, influenced by an individual's pain threshold, past experiences, emotional state, and myriad other factors. For someone with a high pain tolerance, what they rate as a '5' might be another person's '8'. With pain being so multifaceted, navigating its nuances becomes a journey.

It's a journey that requires introspection, resilience, and, most importantly, a quest for understanding. This understanding is what I aim to explore in the subsequent chapters, offering my personal lens on the varying intensities of pain I've encountered and the metamorphosis that ensued. Now, let's dive into my story, beginning with some of my earliest childhood memories.

CHAPTER 1

THE GENESIS OF PAIN

PAIN LEVEL 4

The gentle hum of cicadas filled the still evening air, along with the smell of Union Camp, a familiar backdrop to my little town of Franklin. Among the scattered homes and vast green expanses stood my grandparents' modest house. It felt like a relic from a simpler era, devoid of the conveniences of modern central air or heating. At its core was the cast iron wood heater, its golden warmth acting as the singular shield against the biting cold of winter—a luxury I realized not everyone had. At night, the sound of rain drumming on the tin roof would lull me to sleep; it was nature's very own lullaby.

Our home, as comforting as it was, had its quirks. We had a single bathroom with a floor that seemed to have a mind of its own, sinking in places as if worn out from years of support. The toilet had a constant run, like a babbling brook, and our bathtub, made of solid cast iron, stood vacant of any accompanying shower. Once, during a sleepover at a friend's place, I faced the unfamiliarity of a shower. Embarrassment coursed through me as I fumbled, unsure of how to navigate this luxury that was so commonplace to others yet alien to me.

Our house bore memories and some uninvited guests—roaches. Every so often, one would appear, out of nowhere, in the microwave, the refrigerator, and even my bed. It was a total nightmare to turn the kitchen light on after dark because there were so many of them, at times making my heart sink with embarrassment. The thought of friends visiting and witnessing these intruders always filled me with dread.

Childhood friends became my refuge. We were inseparable, engaging in everything from sports and riding our bikes throughout town to immersing ourselves in music and attending church. Their company was soothing, providing fleeting moments of comfort. Yet, despite their presence, an emptiness lingered within me, a persistent yearning that seemed insurmountable.

One friend stood out among the rest, holding a place in my heart closer than any other. To this day, he remains akin to a brother to me. The laughter we shared and the memories we crafted became a potent antidote to my concealed wounds. He never cast judgment on my living conditions or the dynamics of my family. In truth, the chronicles of our adventures and camaraderie could fill a book of their own. His mother, too, became a maternal figure in my life. She was steadfast and just, embodying strength, wisdom, and a unique sense of humor.

The school playground, ideally a place of joy, was my battlefield. A noticeable tumor on my left shoulder became the source of my nickname: "Hunchback."

My pride and the name-calling led to many fights, which caused me to develop a quick temper. In my mind, if I couldn't beat you now, I would plot on how I would without you ever knowing it. It's astonishing how cruel children can be, their words slicing deeper than the keenest blade. I learned early that not only do sticks and stones hurt, but words also.

In the expansive world of kids with siblings, I felt like a lone wolf. Many times, I found comfort and solace in front of that woodstove beside my grandfather, watching the flames dance their unpredictable tango. It mirrored the unpredictability of my own life. Raised primarily by my grandparents, I grew up faster than most. Psychologists would call this being a "latchkey kid."

Many days, I would return to an empty house, find my hidden key, and fix myself some snacks to eat until one of my grandparents came home. They did everything they could, but both the house and my young heart carried unseen scars. My grandmother had a penchant for thrift store shopping—a ritual I loathed. Growing up, much of my wardrobe comprised of second-hand clothes, and meals often involved the exchange of food stamps. Yet, despite these humble circumstances, my grandparents were adept at showering me with love and correction.

They instilled a sense of pride in me, teaching me to hold my head high. Within the confines of our home, I felt empowered and cherished. It was outside that home where the real challenges lay.

Yet, deeper than the roach-induced shame or the mockery was the echoing void of absence. The place where my father should've stood, the times when my mother seemed to fade away, not even sharing the home I lived in. Occasionally, she'd appear, whisking me away on short adventures, but the true rock in my life was my grandfather, Matthew Cooper.

Saturdays with him were sacred—whether it was grabbing a jelly biscuit from Hardees or taking long drives to North Carolina to breathe in the country air. His pride in me was palpable, his love unconditional. Many of the lessons he instilled remain with me as guiding principles that steer my path. He encouraged me to venture out into the world, always emphasizing the importance of treating others with respect and staying humble.

He was an imposing figure, standing tall at roughly 6 feet 4 inches. If I neglected my chores or failed to learn the lessons he set before me, consequences followed. One of the ringing words he would say was, "Do the work." Being a hardworking man himself, he never made excuses, he himself did the work. Yet, despite the challenges of my youth, he was always there: a listening ear, a source of humor, and a comforting presence.

He and my grandmother were well-known in town — people recognized that when they spoke, they meant every word. As time went on, I underwent surgery to remove a tumor, causing my pronounced hunch. I hoped that after the surgery, people might treat me differently.

But the procedure left a stark scar, about nine or ten inches in length, running across my shoulder blade.

This scar introduced a new challenge to my already complex journey of healing. I felt self-conscious, especially during activities like basketball, where "shirts vs. skins" games would reveal my scar. I often found excuses to avoid such events, fearing the judgment and questions of others. This became a recurring theme throughout my life: How could I conceal my scars? And if someone did notice them, how would I divert their attention or explain them away?" Yet, I recognized that whatever path I chose, dedication and hard work were crucial to success.

Soon after, I decided to immerse myself in karate. My temperament was both an asset and a liability in this endeavor. I detested getting hit, but when it did happen, I'd seethe with anger. My instructor often remarked that my fury was an advantage, suggesting that I needed to be riled up before a tournament because that's when I was at my peak. Initially, this strategy proved successful.

I progressed through the belt ranks and collected numerous trophies — some even taller than me. I began to believe that no one would dare cross me again. Still, as I excelled, the jeers persisted. "Look at the karate kid!" they'd mock, triggering me to retaliate with a punch or kick. Verbally reserved, my actions spoke louder than words.

Back then, I didn't realize that my brawls weren't just about demanding respect.

They were desperate attempts to reclaim a sense of value and self-worth that, in my eyes, was truly acknowledged only by my grandparents. Despite boasting a collection of over 30 trophies in my room, the nights still felt hollow. An extension cord was the sole provider of electricity in my space, and with no heating, the cold seemed to seep into my bones and echo the bleakness I felt within.

The physical coldness was nothing compared to the chilling realization of my grandmother's deteriorating health. She had always been my pillar of strength, the force that held me together through my formative years. Firm in her discipline and abundant in her love, she was instrumental in molding me into the man I would one day become. But a stroke robbed her of her vitality, paralyzing one side of her body and leaving her confined to the sterile environment of a nursing home.

Every visit to that place was a gut-wrenching experience. The strong, vivacious woman I had known all my life now lay there, seemingly defeated. The pungent smell of disinfectant and illness clung to the air, but it was the sight of my Nana, looking so fragile and distant, that was most unbearable. At 16, I struggled to reconcile this image of her with the memories of her vibrant self. I found myself making excuses to avoid the 45-minute drive to see her, unable to confront the painful reality of her condition.

Every missed visit weighed heavily on my conscience, and the guilt was suffocating. She had been there for me unconditionally, and now, when she needed me most, my own vulnerabilities held me back. The pain of seeing her in that state was immense, a testament to the profound bond we shared and the deep love I held for her. It took me years to truly process the loss of her, to come to terms with the void she left behind. The grief was silent, lurking in the shadows, only to hit me when I least expected it.

I still vividly recall the day she passed away. Fresh off the adrenaline of a basketball game, I was driving home, basking in the afterglow of the match. But that euphoria was short-lived. My mom intercepted my car a short distance from my grandparents' house, her face etched with sorrow. When she relayed the news, a piercing pain shot through me, numbing every other sensation.

Without a word, I sped off, not knowing where I was headed. The roads seemed to blur together as tears clouded my vision. For hours, I drove aimlessly, the weight of the loss and the magnitude of the pain becoming my sole companions. With every mile, the realization sank in deeper: it was just me and grandad now. The thought was excruciating.

The anchor of our family, the woman who had been a constant in my life, was gone. The pain wasn't just about losing her; it was about the unspoken words, the visits I had missed, and the guilt of not being there for her when she needed me most.

At the young age of 17, I had accomplished an early high school graduation, accumulating a few college credits along the way. The horizons beyond Franklin beckoned, and I was ready to put distance between my past and my future. As the pages of childhood ended, the pain, while subtle, was ever-present. It was like the distant hum of cicadas during a sultry evening or the gentle rhythm of raindrops on a tin roof. Although one chapter had concluded, my journey was far from over. I stood on the precipice, ready to navigate the vast expanse of experiences and challenges that lay ahead.

CHAPTER 2:

A SOLDIER'S STRIDE

PAIN LEVEL 8

"Marching Orders: The Tolls of Military Life"

The bright sun of South Carolina greeted me daily at Fort Jackson. As a recruit fresh from the comforts of home, the base was an intimidating jungle of discipline, physical rigor, and an unending parade of new faces. This environment starkly contrasted with the warm, familiar surroundings of my grandparents' home in Franklin. Here, in the heart of military training, I was shedding the remnants of the boy I once was, forging ahead into the mold of a soldier. Basic Training introduced its own unique set of hurdles, adding another layer to my transition.

Emerging from a long shower one evening, jeers and laughter greeted me. "Took you long enough!" one soldier called out. Another chimed in, "Acts like he's never had a shower before." Their words stung, a stark reminder of my past. But I wasn't about to divulge my history to them, not here, not now. Instead, I responded the only way I felt would command respect. Striding up to the mocker, I delivered a sharp punch to his face, declaring, "All disrespect stops now! You will respect me."

Chaos ensued as we grappled. The others, caught off guard, watched the unexpected spectacle. Drill sergeants quickly intervened, shouting orders for calm. But the red mist had descended; I couldn't hear them. With each punch, it felt like I was releasing pent-up anger and pain from years of accumulated scars, fighting for my dignity and, perhaps, for a new chapter free from past torment.

As the scuffle ceased, an eerily familiar sentiment echoed in the air. One of the Drill Sergeants, his eyes fixed intently on me, said, "Use it. Channel that rage, soldier." The room, a mix of tension and shock, turned its gaze to the battered soldier, then back to me. The intensity in my eyes silenced any potential whispers. "I'll fight every last one of you," I declared with a raw edge to my voice, my chest heaving.

Many were taken aback. The formerly quiet, smaller recruit had unveiled an unexpected fervor and fire. This newfound reputation soon became my emblem in the unit. It wasn't long before I further asserted this dominance, clinching a victory in one of the pugil stick challenges during a scheduled one-on-one match.

As I stood tall, the foam weapon in my grasp, I felt an adrenaline rush, a sense of invincibility. They had awakened a dormant lion within me, and now, there was no way I was going to let it be tamed. I was ready to roar and claim my place in this new world.

As graduation came it was now time to move on to my next destination. Fort Gordon, Georgia, followed, demanding even more of me. These were the days bereft of the immediate gratifications of social media notifications. Instead, the weight of handwritten letters, with their faint scent of home, were treasures I eagerly awaited. As mail call days passed, it seemed as if nobody had thought to pen me a letter.

I came to a place where I didn't expect to receive anything from loved ones. I remember getting mail from people I had recently met in Fort Jackson. The excitement they had in the letters bridged the gap between my past and present, reminding me of who I once was and cheering on the man I was becoming.

It was at Fort Gordon that I truly transformed. From a wiry boy of 150 pounds, the rigorous training sculpted me into a robust 180-pound man. With every early morning run, every maneuver, and every drill, I felt a renewed sense of belonging. I relished the camaraderie with my fellow soldiers, the collective spirit of resilience, and the shared pride in our blossoming capabilities. In that tight-knit group, "THE FIRM," is what we called it, we found solace.

We had formed an unbreakable bond akin to that of brothers-in-arms. Each of us had a unique story and a different pain, but together, we wove a tapestry of camaraderie. The laughter we shared, the challenges we overcame, and the memories we made became an integral part of my military journey. We would gather around, share tales from home, and discuss dreams of the future. There was power in our collective spirit, and it was evident in how we tackled challenges head-on.

With each passing day, I realized that the bond we had forged was not merely circumstantial. It wasn't just about being in the same location and undergoing the same training. It was deeper than that. It was about understanding each other's pain and being there as a pillar of support, without judgment and without reservation.

As our training neared its end, the reality began to sink in. The impermanence of military life became evident. Our paths, which had converged so beautifully, were about to diverge. The thought of parting ways with my brothers was a heavy one. But such is the nature of service – always on the move, always answering the call of duty. Graduation day was a bittersweet moment. As we stood side by side, pride in our achievements and the anticipation of the journey ahead reflected in our eyes.

Yet underneath it all was the painful realization that the next phase of our lives might not have "the firm" by our side. We promised to stay in touch, to reunite when time allowed, and to always have each other's backs, no matter where our respective duties took us. With heavy hearts but heads held high, we embarked on our individual paths, carrying with us the memories and lessons from our time together.

Upon completion, I found myself in an Army Reserve unit at Fort Lee, Virginia. In many ways, it was very different from the fast-paced training environment I had grown to love. The pace at Fort Lee was languid, and the lack of constant action left me restless. To keep myself engaged, I volunteered for extra days, longing for the military atmosphere that had come to define me. It was during one of these voluntary stints that my Commanding Officer approached me, presenting an opportunity that would determine the course of my military journey.

I found myself at a crossroads after a fruitful summer training at Fort Irwin, California, marred only by the coyotes I had heard tales of. Active duty beckoned, promising adventure and purpose, but it also meant leaving everything familiar behind again. Doubts clouded my mind, amplified by the lukewarm responses from some of my close friends and family. Was I on the right path? Was this new chapter a step forward or a detour?

It was my grandfather, my anchor, who beamed with pride at my decision. To him, my journey was one of courage and honor. Through his eyes, I saw my future unfurling with promise. His friend, a veteran of Pearl Harbor, bestowed upon me wisdom that was both timely and timeless. His tales of bravery, sacrifice, and resilience during that infamous attack illuminated my path, banishing the shadows of doubt.

With renewed vigor, I stepped into the next phase of leaving college life, ready to embrace active duty's challenges and rewards. In the vast expanse of my military journey, I realized I was not just marching toward duty, honor, and service but also toward self-discovery, growth, and understanding. The excitement of the impending duty assignment bubbled within me. With my newfound confidence, I believed I would take the active-duty world by storm, relying on my charisma and enhanced physical abilities. "They aren't ready for me," I often whispered to myself, smirking.

But reality, as it tends to do, came knocking with a surprise of its own. On an early Wednesday morning, the phone rang insistently. Picking it up with an eager heart, I was greeted by the voice of the recruiting officer. "You're heading to Fort Campbell, Kentucky. Report by Monday," he said. Now, I had the audacity to imagine several grand locations for my first assignment, but Kentucky? It was unfamiliar terrain, with President's Day around the corner, and the timing seemed rather inconvenient.

"Where the heck is that?" was my bewildered reaction. A hurried trip to the school library ensued, where I printed out a set of MapQuest directions. Twelve hours away? Well, at least it promised an adventure, I mused, mentally gearing up for the journey ahead. Upon my arrival at Fort Campbell, any notions of smoothly sailing through were quickly dispelled.

The Staff Sergeant in charge was not particularly welcoming, to say the least. She made it clear that I was being assigned to a field artillery unit – another curveball in my rapidly changing trajectory. I attempted to wrap my head around the new information, but more was in store for me. An on-duty Sergeant, with a demeanor gentler than the Staff Sergeant's, led me to the barracks.

I took solace in the fact that I would have a room to myself. A private space to recalibrate after the day's challenges, or so I thought. Little did I know that my room would remain largely unoccupied in the coming days. As it turned out, I had been enrolled in Air Assault

School. Known as the "hardest 11 days in the army", it was a far cry from the initial relaxation I had anticipated.

Training was slated to begin that very Tuesday. Still attempting to acclimate to my new environment, I was overwhelmed. Questions swirled in my mind, unanswered. "I've just arrived," I protested, "This is all happening too fast." With a wry smile, the Sergeant simply responded, "Welcome to active duty."

04:00 hours – the pre-dawn darkness was absolute, interrupted only by the dim outlines of forty soldiers gathered for training. A sharp yell broke the silence, "Fall in!" Our instructor, his voice an unmistakable mix of authority and intimidation, began to address the group. "Not all of you will make it past day zero," he declared, scanning our faces as though challenging us to prove him wrong.

His description of the training ahead was nothing short of daunting. Road marches that escalated in intensity, starting from 6 miles and increasing thereafter, all crammed into an 11-day schedule. I swallowed hard, realizing the magnitude of the challenge that lay ahead. To add to the grueling physical exertion, we were informed of another rule: we had to run. Everywhere! No exceptions!

The days that followed were rigorous and taxing. Sleep was a luxury, and every day, our group dwindled. From forty soldiers, our numbers rapidly shrank to 35, then 25, all within just three days. Yet, a stubborn determination took root within me. "I'm here to stay," I silently pledged to myself.

As the days passed, not only did I endure, but I began to thrive. The final test, a 12-mile road march with a 60-pound rucksack, was daunting. Yet, when we reached the endpoint, I realized I was the second person to finish. A surge of pride welled up within me. I had done it. I was about to graduate and earn the prestigious title of Air Assault, affiliating myself with the renowned Screaming Eagles of the 101st, some of the best soldiers in the land.

The accomplishment invigorated me, pushing me to dream bigger. What would be my next conquest? The Pathfinder course? Airborne? Special Ops! A fire had been lit within me, and there was no stopping it now. "Let's GO!" I roared internally, ready to tackle the next challenge.

I've trained incredibly hard, always aiming for excellence and peak performance. I've transformed from a 180-pound young man to a solid 220 pounds. My bench press max soared to 285 pounds, a testament to my dedication and resilience. And my speed? I could clock two miles in just 11 minutes. As for weapons, my accuracy was unparalleled. I became a machine.

I felt invincible, powerful, and elite. Every ounce of sweat and every hour spent training made me who I am today. It's a journey I'm immensely proud of, a testament to what's possible with sheer determination and a relentless pursuit of excellence.

I remember the pride in my grandfather's eyes when I informed him of my decision to join the army. He held the military in high regard, so seeing his grandson don the uniform was a dream come true for him. Yet, in a bitter twist of fate, the very institution he took pride in kept me away from him during his last moments on earth.

The weight of that missed moment bore down on me heavily. Especially when I realized I was just a week away from a scheduled military leave that would have brought me home. The day of his funeral was a haze. I felt surrounded by murmurs of condolences and whispers of sympathy. But it seemed to me that many didn't truly grasp the depth of the man they were mourning.

Acting on impulse, I ascended the pulpit, taking the place of the minister. Words - raw, anguished, and filled with longing - flowed out of me. It was an outpouring of emotions, driven by grief and the sharp pang of regret. A wish for one last conversation, one last lesson, one last embrace. Yet life, in all its unpredictability, had carved out a different path for me.

Fast forward a few years, and I had grown accustomed to the demanding rhythm of Army life. The challenges were intense, but so were the rewards. With rapid promotions, accolades, and a reputation for excellence, my military career was on an upward trajectory. Life had settled into a predictable yet fulfilling pattern. These were the days of revelry, venturing into the unknown, and testing the limits of my youth.

The "Wild N Out" crew wasn't just about parties and fast cars; it was also a testament to our resilient spirit. Amid the raucous laughter and adrenaline-pumping escapades, we were learning to navigate the challenges of life away from home, relying on each other for support. For many of us, this was our first taste of true freedom, and we embraced it with all the zeal of our young hearts.

It wasn't just the camaraderie, shared jokes, or adventures that bonded us—it was the unwavering trust we placed in each other. I felt the weight of their expectations, not as a burden but as an honor. They saw in me a leader, someone they could rally behind, and that was a mantle I carried with pride and responsibility. Through thick and thin, highs and lows, their loyalty never wavered, and neither did mine. In our shared moments of joy, sorrow, or challenge, the unspoken promise was always clear: "I've got you." And that mutual assurance became the bedrock of our bond.

"A man who has friends must himself be friendly, but there is a friend who sticks closer than a brother." - Proverbs 18:24 (NKJV)

During these whirlwind days, I sought to weave threads of my upbringing, a touch of traditional values, into our modern adventures. The stipulation to attend church on Sunday mornings was initially met with reluctant sighs and playful grumbles, but in time, it became a silent pact among us. One of my friends who did attend openly accepted Jesus in his life. The thing is, he had never been to church before, and he had asked me time and time again to go. Perhaps, beneath all our youthful defiance, we all sensed a deep-seated need for that spiritual grounding, especially when navigating the stormy seas of our hedonistic pursuits.

Late nights faded into early mornings, and our group thrived on the adrenaline of anticipating the next weekend's escapades. It was in one of these vibrant interludes that I first encountered alcohol. It wasn't just a brief introduction; it felt more like a turbulent tumble down a rabbit hole, with a dazzling array of choices beckoning from every corner. Yet, amidst the haze of intoxication, the call of duty always served as a grounding force, pulling me back to sobriety when needed.

Despite the deep bond, there were moments when I felt isolated in my own thoughts. As the music blared and laughter filled the air, I would sometimes drift into a reverie, the weight of my past pulling me into its depths. But the beauty of our group was that I was never left to drown in my thoughts for long. A hand would reach out, pulling me back into the present, reminding me that I wasn't alone in this journey.

"Wild N Out" became more than just a name; it became our mantra, our declaration to the world that no matter the challenges we faced, we would confront them head-on with unwavering spirit and unbreakable bonds. But the rapid pace of our lives, the thirst for the next thrill, couldn't last forever. Change was on the horizon, even if we were blissfully unaware of its impending approach.

That pivotal morning forever etched in history, 9 am on September 11th, still echoes in my ears. Having just concluded a relentless 24-hour shift and with ambitions set on transitioning into special operations, I was unprepared for the jarring news that pierced through: America was under siege. In an instant, the military base transformed, with alarms sounding and a palpable tension that one could almost touch. We stood on the precipice of war. And in that profound moment, our group dynamics, our festive parties, and all our laid-out plans were abruptly eclipsed. Duty beckoned.

"In preparing for battle, I have always found that plans are useless, but planning is indispensable."
- General Dwight D. Eisenhower

From a haven of achievement, my world suddenly tilted into chaos. The tragic events of that fateful day would eventually lead my boots to the sands of Iraq. Prepared as I was, with sharp skills, keen knowledge of weaponry, and a robust team beside me, I soon learned that preparation can only shield you so much. Life has a way of throwing curveballs that can knock even the most prepared off their feet.

The reality of war's brutality struck almost immediately upon our arrival in Iraq when one of my closest battle buddies was killed. The bubble of invincibility shattered, revealing the fragile nature of human existence. The shadow of fear constantly lingered, and the specter of death became a regular companion. In the midst of war, there's the ever-present awareness that each breath might be your last. Such experiences reshape your perspective on life.

"Courage is fear holding on a minute longer."
- General George S. Patton

My faith in Jesus became the beacon that guided me through the darkest nights. Throughout my service in Iraq, I endured physical injuries; shrapnel peppered my arms and back, a testament to the peril we faced daily. Beyond the tangible injuries, the psychological scars burrowed profoundly. Two concussions from blasts resulted in head traumas that evolved into persistent headaches that wouldn't stop. This pain was as mentally debilitating as it was physically excruciating.

Being sidelined by these injuries, I felt an overwhelming sense of guilt and helplessness. Our team was tight-knit, with each member bringing a unique skill set to the table. Being unable to perform my duties felt like a betrayal, even if it was out of my control. Everything seemed to be disintegrating around me. The vibrant soldier, ready to take on the world, felt trapped in a body that was failing him and a mind clouded with pain and doubt.

But pain has a way of teaching resilience, of showing you depths of strength you never knew existed. As with every challenge before this, I was determined to find my way to the other side of this pain. After being diagnosed with chronic migraines, which significantly affected my ability to be effective in combat, it became clear that my time on the front lines was ending.

Having sustained multiple injuries, the persistent effects of the head trauma were the most daunting. Two grueling deployments and 19 months later, I was being sent back to the States. The weight of disappointment, a new kind of pain, pressed on me. But the battles weren't over; they had only changed form.

After an exhausting three-day journey that included a layover in Kuwait, where I endured a sweltering 120-degree heat while held up in a tent, my conditions became all the more challenging. Being on medications and grappling with migraines in such an environment was a test of my endurance. However, the long flight route from Kuwait finally culminated in my arrival in Norfolk, Virginia.

The relief of being back on American soil was palpable, and I cherished the two-week respite before the call of duty beckoned me once again. I recall stepping into the airport and instantly met with a heartwarming sight. Families were everywhere, joyously welcoming their soldiers back with flowers, balloons, heartfelt embraces, joyous laughter, and tears of relief. I scanned the crowd, searching for a familiar face.

"Where's mom? Is anyone here for me?" I pondered, feeling a pinch in my heart. Having just returned from the harrowing experiences of a combat zone, the silence of my own reception stung deeply. As I watched soldier after soldier leave with their loved ones, I was left alone with nothing but my duffle bag as company. A mix of tears and anger welled up inside me. "They couldn't even come to the airport," I thought, trying to hold back the flood of emotions.

Eventually, I reached out to a cousin of mine who was working at a barbershop in a nearby city. Without hesitation, he left work and drove to the airport to pick me up. I waited at the airport for what felt like an eternity but was roughly two hours. The sight of a familiar face was immensely comforting. The hum of his SUV and his welcoming smile radiated warmth. "What's up, 'coop'? Welcome home," he greeted me. Hearing those words was a balm to my soul.

However, as we embarked on the hour-long drive home, I couldn't shake the feeling that something within me had fundamentally changed. I was no longer the same person who left these shores. The sights and sounds of the bustling city that once felt familiar now seemed distant and alien. The radio chatter, passing billboards, even the honking of the horns - they all felt like remnants of a life I had left behind.

As we drove, my cousin tried to fill the silence with stories of home, but my mind was elsewhere. Each word he spoke was a stark reminder of the chasm that had grown between the world I now knew and the world I had left behind. The laughter and banter at the barbershop, the neighborhood gossip, and the latest music seemed trivial compared to the life-and-death realities I had just lived through.

I caught my reflection in the side mirror. The face that stared back was not that of the eager young man who had left for deployment. It was a face etched with the weariness of battle, the lines of stress, and the shadows of memories best forgotten. Memories of comrades lost, decisions made in the heat of the moment, and the sounds and smells of war that would haunt my dreams for years to come.

Arriving home, the familiar surroundings of my childhood seemed like a mirage. I had yearned for this moment, to be back in the embrace of family and the comforts of home. But now that I was here, a sense of dislocation washed over me. My mom was at work, and so was my stepdad. My hopes of them taking the day off vanished. I was back, but I wasn't really "home". The journey to find my way back to myself had just begun.

A creeping realization dawned on me: Was this fear? Why were my hands trembling? Why did sudden sweats drench me? Ordinary noises now felt jarringly loud, flashing lights induced severe migraines, and bouts of dizziness would seize me without warning. What was happening to me?

To make matters more challenging, family members seemed eager to hear about my time overseas, treating it like some video game adventure. Comments like, "It's just a headache," or, "It couldn't have been that bad over there," stoked a fire of anger within me. While they lounged comfortably in their homes, I had faced unspeakable horrors every day. I witnessed death, not only of fellow soldiers but also of innocent civilians, including children.

There were things I had to do, unthinkable choices I had to make in the name of survival. To them, it might seem like just another day, but for me, each day was a renewed battle against my traumas and memories. Scars seemed to have a voice of their own, echoing memories, pain, and fear into my daily life. My mind was a battlefield, with every small trigger or sound rekindling the traumas I'd faced. As I tried to reintegrate into life, the chasm between my past and my present widened. It felt like walking in a maze of mirrors, where every reflection showed a version of me that I both recognized and didn't.

"War leaves a void that's hard to fill."- Lt. Col. Jay

The comforts of home, which I had longed for during my deployments, now seemed foreign and disorienting. Simple tasks became challenges. Conversations became minefields, with the potential to stray into topics or memories I wasn't ready to confront. And then there were the dreams—vivid, horrifying replays that jolted me awake in the darkness, drenched in sweat.

It wasn't just the war stories that weighed on me. It was the looks of pity or misunderstanding, the unsolicited advice, the stark reminders that while I had changed, the world around me had carried on without me. Shadows of my past followed me everywhere, and the echoes of gunshots, cries, and haunting memories played on repeat in my mind.

As I navigated this new reality, I began to wonder: Could I ever find a place where the shadows were merely shadows and the echoes silent? Would there ever be a time when I could walk in the sunlight without being haunted by my past? Each day brought its challenges, but with it, the hope that maybe, just maybe, I could move beyond the phantoms of my history. I longed for clarity, purpose, and a reason to believe that the scars of yesteryears could be replaced by the aspirations of tomorrow.

As the days passed, an unexpected twist arrived. I received an email from my branch. Opening it, I found new marching orders: a directive to report back to the military installation. My heart raced. It wasn't just a return to duty; it hinted at the promise of being thrust back into action, into the thick of it all. A chance to be fully engaged again, to feel the pulsating rhythm of a mission, and perhaps, to find solace in the purpose it provided.

This was it – an opportunity to reshape my narrative. As I packed my bags, preparing to respond to the call, I felt a mix of anticipation and determination. This new chapter awaited me, and I was ready to pen it with vigor and hope.

Chapter 3

Fractured Familiarity

Pain Level 9

"Shadows and Echoes"

As I arrived on base and checked in, a sense of uncertainty washed over me. The military had seen its fair share of soldiers coming in and out, but my situation felt unique — a soldier with commendable credentials now marred by undeniable disabilities. Instead of a clear assignment, I was handed a profile — "a medical assessment that seemingly restricted me in every possible way."

My orders were simple, almost disarmingly so. Call in for a morning check-in and ensure I attended all medical appointments. That was it. No drills, no missions, no field exercises. This wasn't the active duty I had envisioned for myself. It was far removed from the bustling, adrenaline-pumping activities of a base in full swing. Instead, it felt stagnant, almost like a pause in a movie, waiting for someone to hit the play button.

Each morning, as the sun's first rays broke the horizon, the familiar sound of soldiers running in formation, their voices unified in rhythmic cadence, filled the air. It was a melody of discipline, camaraderie, and purpose — a song I once knew by heart. I yearned to be out there, to be part of that synchronized dance of boots hitting the ground. But every time I even contemplated the idea, a sharp sting of pain would jolt me back to reality, a cruel reminder of my limitations.

Most days, the weight of my disabilities felt like a leaden blanket, pinning me down and rendering me immobile. The confines of my quarters became both a sanctuary and a prison. While the walls shielded me from the pitying glances of others, they also echoed back my frustrations and regrets. It was a stark contrast to the vibrant, active soldier I once was. Now, I was trapped, not just by my physical limitations but by the chains of longing for what once was and the uncertainty of what lay ahead.

The migraines, constant reminders of the injuries and trauma, persisted. My experiences in Iraq hadn't just left physical scars but had imprinted deep emotional ones. These reverberations from the past clouded my everyday life, casting shadows on moments that should've been light-filled. The journey to healing, understanding, and reclaiming my sense of self was about to take on new dimensions.

These new dimensions took the form of sterile doctor's offices, the familiar chime of pharmacy doors, and the ceaseless rattle of pill bottles. Every visit was accompanied by the hope that the next medication would be the panacea, the miracle cure to mend what felt broken. Instead, each appointment seemed to append to a growing list of diagnoses and prescriptions.

How had it come to this? Once a beacon of health and resilience, I now grappled with a body that felt foreign, betraying me at every turn. My identity as a soldier, someone who had faced insurmountable odds on the battlefield and emerged victorious, was now no comparison against this version of me – vulnerable, defeated, shackled by the very flesh and bone that once served as my armor.

The weight of it all turned me to the numbing embrace of alcohol. Every drink was a desperate attempt to drown the cacophony of thoughts that threatened my sanity. The accolades, the commendations, the pride – did they mean nothing if my body and mind refused to cooperate? The idea of having to possibly return to Franklin was haunting. It wasn't just about geography; it symbolized defeat, regression, and a return to a place and time I felt I had outgrown.

The phrase "this is your new normal" was introduced to me during one particularly harrowing visit to the clinic. It was presented as a form of acceptance, an acknowledgment that life had irrevocably changed. But I resisted it. To accept this as my "new normal" felt like relinquishing control, surrendering to a fate I didn't choose. However, as the medications piled up and my symptoms persisted, it became harder to refute the reality staring me in the face.

Determined, I held onto hope, even as shadows lengthened and the world blurred around the edges. The journey to reclaiming myself from the depths of despair was fading. Life's pain was no longer just a dull ache; it had intensified, reaching the higher echelons of the scale, hitting levels of 8,9 and even 10. Alcohol was no longer a mere companion; it became the lifeblood that pulsed through my veins, mingling dangerously with the potent narcotics doctors had prescribed.

The world outside, once teeming with opportunities and adventures, had faded into a distant blur. The cocktail of substances meant to provide relief was imprisoning me in a haze, creating a chasm between the real world and me. Most days, I felt more specter than human, drifting aimlessly through the motions.

It wasn't just substances that I clung to; the hollow company of fleeting relationships became another crutch. Each new face, each warm embrace, was a temporary balm on a wound that refused to heal. It was an attempt to rekindle a semblance of worthiness, to feel desired, even if just for a moment. But with each dawn, the emptiness would return, more profound than before.

Besides years prior, I had gone through my first divorce. I was young, 20 years old, and the rigor of military and life desisted us. One of the things I knew my mom wasn't going to like, and dealing with rejection so much early in life, this was just another blow. This only added to the shame and thought of failure I was accumulating.

> *"We have this hope as an anchor for the soul, firm and secure. It enters the inner sanctuary behind the curtain." Hebrews 6:19*

In this scripture, hope is described as an anchor for the soul, suggesting that just as an anchor stabilizes a ship, our hope in God and His promises provides stability and security to our lives. In the middle of this tempestuous sea of self-destruction stood an unlikely anchor: my faith. Yes, during the chaos, I still reached out for the soothing pages of my Bible, the words of hope a stark contrast to my reality.

It may sound like a paradox, this contrast of a downward spiral and the relentless pursuit of divine comfort. Yet, every Sunday, with my body riddled with pain, I would drag my fractured self to the church. The familiar hymns and sermons were small pockets of solace in a world that seemed increasingly alien.

Despite the external chaos, internally, one thought persisted: "I am still a soldier." That belief, that kernel of identity, kept the hope of recovery alive. It was the thread, however thin, that kept me from completely unraveling. The journey to reclaim not just my health but my soul was proving harder than any battlefield I'd faced, but I wasn't ready to wave the white flag just yet.

Each visit to a new doctor or therapist felt like a new chapter in a book that I didn't want to read. The sterile smell of hospitals became too familiar. The glaring lights of examination rooms made my migraines flare even more. Medical brochures, filled with jargon and illustrations, became the backdrop of my life.

One doctor described PTSD (Post Traumatic Stress Disorder) as if it were just a file in a cabinet. For me, it felt like a torrential storm, unpredictable and overpowering. Another explained Chronic Migraines as having a pain threshold that was continuously being breached, like an alarm that wouldn't turn off. Sleep Apnea wasn't just a sleeping disorder. Every time I woke up gasping, it was a cruel reminder of the life-threatening situations I'd faced in Iraq.

Vertigo, they said, was a matter of balance. Yet, to me, it felt like the ground was continuously being pulled from under my feet, sending me into a relentless spiral of disorientation. Plantar fasciitis, the inflammation in the feet, made every step a searing reminder of the miles I'd trekked across rugged terrains, often with a heavy pack. The anxiety wasn't just a feeling of nervousness; it felt like a vice grip on my chest, turning each breath into a painful, laborious effort.

The hair loss, a cruel side effect of one of the many medications I was on, was a daily visual reminder of how my body seemed to be betraying me, piece by piece. To add insult to injury, even my sex drive, something so integral to personal identity and intimate relationships, dwindled. A combination of physical pain, emotional turmoil, and the cocktail of medications I was on seemed to sap away at that part of me too.

It wasn't just about the act; it was about losing another piece of normalcy, another reminder of everything that had changed. The emotional toll was mirrored in my physical appearance. From a strong, toned figure of 220 pounds, my weight plummeted to a gaunt 163. To make matters worse, the stark transformation drew concerned glances, further magnifying my inner struggles. The once robust and energetic version of me was replaced by a reflection that looked weary and drained, bearing silent testimony to the battles I was fighting within.

Therapists suggested journaling, deep breathing exercises, and group therapy. I tried them all, looking for a lifeline, a hint of relief. Some techniques provided momentary solace, while others seemed pointless. Group therapy was a mixed bag. On one hand, there was solace in knowing I wasn't alone. But on the other, every shared story added to the weight of collective trauma, making the world seem even darker.

As if the emotional weight wasn't burdensome enough, there was the daily medication routine, a cocktail of over 13 pills three times a day. These were meant to keep me anchored, but they came with their own storm of side effects. Nosebleeds became a frequent, unwelcome visitor, staining sheets and handkerchiefs alike. Nightmares haunted my nights, forcing me to relive the horrors over and over. Some days, the crushing weight of it all made me retreat to dark rooms, where silence and shadows provided a temporary refuge from the relentless pain.

The medicine was supposed to rebuild the bridge between my fragmented memories and the present, but often, they seemed to further distort it. My reality was fractured into pieces, like a mirror shattered into countless shards, each reflecting a distorted, painful image of what once was. Every day was a struggle, a constant battle between seeking normalcy and succumbing to the chaos within.

What became clear was that pain wasn't just a sensation. It was a complex interplay of physical discomfort, emotional turmoil, and mental distress. The pain scale, from 1 to 10, that doctors often referred to felt too linear, too simplistic. My pain was multidimensional, fluctuating between past traumas, present challenges, and fears of the future.

However, amidst this overwhelming tapestry of pain and diagnoses, there was a glimmer of hope. Every medical professional I met, every therapist session I attended, and every support group I joined was a testament to my resilience and determination. It was a search, a relentless pursuit of the other side of pain, where healing and peace awaited. I often looked at my reflection, searching for the soldier who once felt invincible, but instead, all I saw was a broken man trying to piece himself together. But within that shattered image, there was a spark, a will to fight, and the knowledge that even in the darkest hours, there's always a dawn waiting to break.

The steadfast love of the Lord never ceases; his mercies never come to an end; they are new every morning; great is your faithfulness."
Lamentations 3:22-23

This journey was not just about battling the pain but about finding oneself amidst the chaos. I realized that pain wasn't the enemy; it was merely a teacher pushing me to discover my strengths, teaching me patience, resilience, and the power of perseverance. Even though some days felt like an endless night, I held onto the belief that every sunrise brought a new day, a new beginning, and a chance to rewrite my story. As I move forward, I carry with me not just the scars of my past but also the lessons they've taught me. The road to recovery might be long and winding, but I am determined to walk it, one step at a time, with hope in my heart and faith in the journey.

Chapter 4

Muted Celebrations

Pain Level 8

"A heavy heart, a mix of sadness and longing, like the pain that lingers after a deep cut begins to heal."

The days before had been a blur, consumed by my internal struggles and the weight of my thoughts. But as I sat in that moment of introspection, the unexpected sound of my phone pierced the silence. I hesitated for a split second before answering. The familiar voice on the other end belonged to my Company Commander, a man I held in high regard.

"Come to formation tomorrow," he instructed, his voice betraying a hint of enthusiasm that piqued my curiosity. There was an undertone of something positive, but he kept the details to himself. "Just be there," he added, leaving me in suspense. Hanging up the phone, a flurry of thoughts raced through my mind. What could this be about? Was this the turning point I had been hoping for?

For the first time in what felt like ages, a sense of anticipation bubbled within me. This call, so unexpected in its timing, felt like God's way of telling me that change was on the horizon. The shadows of my past experiences were still present, but now there was a glimmer of something else—a potential shift in the narrative of my life. As the day transitioned into night, my mind started crafting countless scenarios of what the following day would bring.

The morning sun streamed through the window, casting a golden glow on the room. The anticipation from the night before still hung in the air as I prepared myself for the formation. The thought of what lay ahead filled me with a mix of anxiety and hope. Amidst the whirlwind of emotions, I clung to the belief that maybe, just maybe, things were turning around. As the sunlight painted a new day, I decided to face it head-on, armed with hope and the potential of a new beginning.

Standing tall amidst the regimented lines, I felt the familiar sense of pride every time I wore the uniform—a representation of honor, duty, and sacrifice. Today, however, there was an added layer: the hope that my sacrifices and struggles had been recognized. As the commander emerged, his presence immediately commanded respect. All eyes were on him. And then, without much preamble, he called me out. Every fiber of my being was on high alert.

"Congratulations," he exclaimed, pride evident in his voice, "You made the list." Those words brought an overwhelming wave of emotion. Promotion was the furthest thing from my mind in the recent past, but now, it felt like a beacon of acknowledgment. The assembly dispersed with congratulatory pats on the back and a few teasing remarks from my comrades.

However, the commander's additional request to see me lingered in my mind. My heart raced, thoughts swirling in confusion and anticipation. His office felt a bit colder than the outside, perhaps symbolic of the unknown news I was about to receive. As the door clicked shut behind me, his somber demeanor was unmistakable.

"First, congratulations again," he started, pausing for a moment as if to weigh his words. "But there's something else. The hospital needs to see you. It's urgent." My heart sank. What more could it possibly be? Doubts and fears resurfaced. Still, I was a soldier, trained to face challenges head-on, so I nodded, masking the turmoil inside.

The atmosphere in the hospital was markedly different. The human resources lead, with her aghast expression, seemed like she was about to deliver life-altering news. And she did. "Your retirement has been approved. Effective immediately."

It felt as if the room had been sucked of all its air. Panic rose in my chest as the weight of her words settled. Retirement? Now? So soon? The questions raced, and yet no answers came forth. "Why? How?" I stammered. The thoughts of settling into a promotion, regaining my place, and serving with pride seemed to dissipate instantly. She tried to explain, pointing to some paperwork and mentioning urgent directives, but it all seemed a blur.

"Life is about change. Sometimes it's painful, sometimes it's beautiful, but most of the time, it's both."
– Kristin Kreuk

The quote echoed in my mind, reminding me of the unpredictability of life's journey. Retirement was never part of my immediate plan. I had visualized a return, a resurgence. I was on track to be a Sergeant Major(E9) by the age of 38/39. Now, a different path lay ahead—a life without the comradeship, without the uniform.

As the initial shock wore off, I tried to see the silver lining. Retirement meant time—time to heal, time to rediscover myself, time to embark on a new journey. But was I ready? Only time would tell. The transition had begun. The day had been a whirlwind of emotions, from the unexpected high of a promotion to the baffling revelation of my imminent retirement. As if fate had one more twist in store, I found myself back at the formation grounds, the sun now descending, casting long shadows on the familiar parade square.

The atmosphere was thick with anticipation. My comrades exchanged curious glances; whispers spread like wildfire. "Is he getting promoted again?" someone joked, but the levity of the comment didn't reach me. My heart thudded loudly in my chest, echoing the anxiety and uncertainty I felt.

As I stepped forward, the specialist, with a ceremonial tone, began reading the official letter of my retirement. Each word felt like a sharp sting, an undeniable reality that I had to come to terms with. Around me, I could sense the shock, the disbelief. The same men I had trained with, fought alongside, and shared countless memories with were now struggling to wrap their heads around this unforeseen turn of events.

The formalities continued, but my mind was elsewhere, grappling with a future I hadn't anticipated. How do you condense a lifetime of service, memories, and bonds into a mere ten days? The thought was overwhelming. When the formation disbanded, some approached with words of consolation, others with admiration for the service I had rendered, and a few with tears in their eyes. Their reactions mirrored the gamut of emotions I was experiencing: sadness, pride, confusion, and hope.

Over the next few days, the process of out-processing became a blur of paperwork, medical evaluations, and farewell ceremonies. Every handshake, every salute, every shared memory was a poignant reminder of the life I was leaving behind. But amidst the chaos, a realization slowly emerged.

Life often throws curveballs and challenges that test our mettle and our resilience. With every ending comes a new beginning, a chance to reinvent oneself and find a renewed purpose. The military had been my identity, my world. But now I was on the brink of a new chapter, one where the lessons learned in uniform would guide me in navigating the challenges ahead. So, with a heavy heart but an unwavering spirit, I embarked on my new journey, ready to face whatever the future held with the same courage, determination, and resilience that the military had instilled in me.

The shadows of the day seemed to follow me as night approached. The duality of emotions - from the joy of promotion to the abrupt realization of retirement - now felt like a distant memory as an old adversary reared its head. Pain. It always had a way of sneaking up, pulling me into its clutches when least expected.

In search of temporary relief, I turned to an all-too-familiar concoction: the tangy taste of a Long Island mixed with the numbing effects of morphine and rest from melatonin. The mix, although dangerous, had been a solace in past times of anguish. But that night, the cocktail's repercussions were magnified. Instead of providing the expected comfort, it intensified the pain, making it feel as if a vice was tightening around my head. I dialed 911. I need help. I recall saying, I think I'm dying. My screams echoed through the sterile hallways as the medical staff rushed me in.

In that cold, indifferent hospital room, solitude became my only companion once again. The machines beeped in rhythm to my racing heart, and the coldness of the bed served as a cruel reminder of the isolation I felt. Time and again, pain had become an unwelcome guest, forcing me to face it alone. Every recurrence made me question the cards I had been dealt. "Is this my life now?" I wondered, the weight of that thought pressing down.

Two days later brought not just light but two stern-faced doctors. One discussed the debilitating nature of my migraines, pointing out their alarming resemblance to stroke symptoms. My face was drooped and was numb. The words floated around, but the weight of the next doctor's message hit hard. His eyes locked onto mine, devoid of the usual clinical detachment. "You have to stop drinking alcohol; with the medication you're on, it's a deadly cocktail." It's going to kill you!

Alcohol had become my crutch, my means of escaping a reality that felt too heavy to bear. The bitter realization that even this small escape was now off-limits was crushing. Everything that provided even a semblance of relief seemed to be slipping through my fingers. The words I yelled in the hospital were not PG-13 friendly.

Yet, amidst the whirlwind of emotions, a glimmer of clarity emerged. The doctor's words were not just a warning; they were a lifeline, an opportunity. An opportunity to confront my pain, not numb it; to face my challenges, not escape them; and to find genuine healing, not temporary relief. I had to "do the work".

The road ahead was undeniably daunting. But with every challenge comes an opportunity for growth. I had faced countless battles in my military career and life. This was just another battle, albeit of a different kind. With the same resilience, determination, and courage that had carried me through the toughest times, I was ready to face this head-on.

The emotions from the past few days had left me disoriented, and the glaring realities of my immediate future were now impossible to ignore. With no academic credentials completed, dwindling finances, bad credit, and the looming uncertainty of a roof over my head, I was at a crossroads, facing challenges I had never anticipated. I had two months of leave saved for transition. I was going to need it.

An offer of temporary refuge came from an unexpected source. Someone I had met a few weeks back, aware of my predicament, extended an invitation to stay with her for a short while. "Just until you find your footing," she had said with an encouraging smile. The offer seemed innocent enough, a lifeline in my stormy sea. A couple of weeks, I thought. It'll give me time to figure things out.

Even as that thought gave me a semblance of relief, there was one call I had been dreading, a conversation that brought a different kind of pain—my mother. The thought of returning to Franklin, admitting defeat, and seeking refuge in the familiarity of my hometown was daunting. The weight of potential judgment and the fear of being perceived as a failure pressed heavily on me.

I dialed the familiar number, heart pounding. The ring seemed to echo the anxiety I felt. Her voice now made my throat tighten. Gathering all the courage I could muster, I let the words tumble out, "Mom, can I come stay with you for a while?"
The pause on the other end felt like an eternity. Each silent second amplified my feelings of shame and vulnerability. And then she replied, "Yes."

The relief was short-lived, as she followed with the question I was ill-prepared to answer, "What will you do next?" The real answer was a maze of uncertainty and fear. But admitting that, unveiling my scars and raw vulnerabilities, seemed too much. So, I did what I had become adept at: I masked my uncertainties with a veneer of confidence. "I've got a job lined up," I lied, hoping that this facade would buy me time to figure out my next move and rebuild my life. Deep down, I knew that this was just a temporary reprieve. The road to finding my new purpose and truly healing was only just beginning.

Those next few weeks came with a heaviness that seemed to permeate the air. Packing up my belongings was a symbolic act. I was not just leaving behind a physical space but also a chapter of my life that held mixed memories of pain, hope, and transitions. As I zipped up the last of my bags, I took a deep breath, steeling myself for the journey ahead.

A 12-hour drive lay before me, a journey not just of distance but of introspection. The road would take me through familiar terrains and landscapes that held memories of a younger, more carefree version of myself. But today, they would be seen through the tear-blurred eyes of a man who had faced the harshest realities of life and was now returning to his roots in search of solace and a fresh start.

As I loaded my Tahoe, I looked up at my friend's house; our last meeting was still fresh in my mind. The temptation to go in, to say a proper goodbye, was strong. But I hesitated. We were at two different crossroads in life, and sometimes, a silent departure speaks volumes. I ghosted, thinking it was for the best. We were both heading in different directions and maybe, just maybe, some goodbyes are better left unsaid.

The roar of the car's engine broke the night's silence as I began the drive. The road stretched endlessly ahead, the horizon blurry from my tears. Every mile I covered seemed to be a step back in time but also a step towards hope, healing, and new beginnings.

> *"Behind every brave face is a broken heart, but within that heart also lies the strength to rebuild and rise again." Dr. Shumonte Cooper*

As the familiar landmarks of my hometown started appearing, signaling the end of my long drive, I realized that this was not an end but a new beginning.

CHAPTER 5

SCARS OF SERVICE: NAVIGATING THE TERRAIN OF RETURN

PAIN LEVEL 10

The familiarity of my childhood hometown, which once evoked warmth and nostalgia, now felt foreign. The walls echoed with silent judgments, or at least, that's how it felt. The faces I encountered daily seemed to bear an unspoken question, an unsaid pity, that magnified my sense of inadequacy.

I yearned for the reassuring touch of a mother, for her to simply hold me and say, "I'm proud of you" or "I support you and have your back." I wished for a safe space where I could unveil my vulnerabilities without fear. But that comfort seemed elusive. I defaulted to the mask I had mastered, the "I'm okay" facade that belied the storm within. Every conversation and interaction was punctuated by my feigned optimism, even as my soul screamed in silence.

Each evening, as they went about their routines, I would retreat to the solitude of my room. The bed, which should have been a haven, became my prison. Alone with my thoughts and pain, I felt isolated in a house full of people. Conversations about my pain felt like throwing words into a void, where they would just dissipate without making an impact.

Days turned into weeks, then months. The medication rendered me numb, a shadow of my former self. The daily pill regimen remained a cruel reminder of my fractured existence. As I looked in the mirror, my eyes, though surrounded by smiles, seemed to scream, "Help me." My pleas, silent as they were, went unnoticed. The weight of my internal strife reached its peak one fateful Saturday night.

Lying in bed, with pain ricocheting through my mind and body, the desperate idea took root. "Enough is enough," I whispered through gritted teeth, tears streaming down my face. The bottle of hydrocodone lay ominously on the nightstand. In a haze of despair, I swallowed pill after pill, hoping to end the relentless agony. My final thought as darkness encroached was a desperate plea, "Lord, if you won't take this pain, I will."

To my astonishment, sunlight pierced my eyes the next morning. I was alive. A mix of disbelief and fear coursed through me. Amid the overwhelming emotions, there was clarity. I needed healing, not just physically but spiritually. I dressed in haste as a singular thought propelled me forward: "I need to find a church." The spiritual void in me yearned for a connection, a touch of divine intervention.

I needed to be surrounded by faith, hope, and prayers. Today, more than ever, I needed to believe in miracles and redemption. From an early age, religion had been my compass. It provided answers to life's mysteries, gave solace in trying times, and built a community of shared values and beliefs. My faith was the lens through which I saw the world, offering clarity and purpose.

As my journey within my faith progressed, it became apparent that the bedrock of my beliefs was shifting. The religious tenets I'd held onto for stability seemed more like quicksand, dragging me into a spiritual abyss. Questioning and doubt, rather than being fleeting thoughts, had taken center stage. They were not merely intellectual queries but profound, soul-wrenching interrogations.

I found solace in the words of a famed theologian, who once remarked, "Doubt isn't the opposite of faith; it is an element of faith." It made me realize that my spiritual crisis wasn't a sign of weak faith but perhaps an invitation to deepen it. In the depths of despair, scripture has a way of illuminating the path back to hope.

As I pondered my next steps, words from the Bible that spoke of forgiveness and redemption resonated deeply within me. "If we confess our sins, he is faithful and just to forgive us our sins and to cleanse us from all unrighteousness." - 1 John 1:9. This scripture whispered the promise of a clean slate, reminding me that no matter how far I felt I had strayed, God's arms remained open, waiting for my return.

"Come to me, all you who are weary and burdened, and I will give you rest." - Matthew 11:28

This invitation to find solace in the divine resonated profoundly. It promised not just rest for the body but for the soul – a deep, rejuvenating peace that I so desperately craved. Armed with this newfound hope, I immersed myself in the church community. The sermons, the prayers, and the shared experiences all became stepping stones towards my spiritual renewal. It wasn't just about attending services; it was about forging a deep, personal relationship with Jesus and reigniting the faith that had once been the cornerstone of my life.

I rededicated my life to Jesus, making a conscious choice to start afresh. The church became my sanctuary, a place where my brokenness was acknowledged but also where healing began. The love, acceptance, and guidance I received helped piece together the fragmented parts of my soul.

The silver lining, it seemed, was not just in the renewed relationship with God but in the profound realization that no matter the depths of one's despair, there's always a way back to light, love, and peace. My journey was a testament to the enduring power of faith and the limitless capacity of God's love to heal and restore. I also knew I still had a journey ahead that would not be smooth sailing.

Determined to be consistent with my new commitment, I yearned for deeper knowledge and a stronger connection. My spiritual hunger led me to enroll at Liberty University to pursue a theology degree. This decision stemmed from a mix of emotional pain and a deep-seated desire to understand God's word more thoroughly.

As I delved into my studies, I found myself absorbing the teachings voraciously, filling the voids within me. My passion for sharing the gospel with others grew intensely, and my zeal for Christ's teachings was evident to all around me. This transformative period culminated in my licensing as a minister—a calling I'd never envisioned for myself.

Yet, amidst these triumphant milestones, internal battles persisted. The duality of my spiritual ascent and the lurking shadows of past trauma made for a complex internal landscape. One of the most challenging parts was feeling isolated in my struggles. While I had a deep connection with God and the scriptures, finding peers who could truly empathize with the tumult of my journey was rare. The road ahead, I realized, would be one of continued healing, seeking understanding, and the perpetual quest for true fellowship.

The expectations I had set for myself and the perceptions surrounding the ministry weighed heavily on me. Every minister around me seemed flawless, an embodiment of righteousness and virtue. Only a few were like true brothers to me, engaging in genuine conversations that reflected the challenges of real life. However, the majority remained oblivious to my tumultuous past. In their eyes, I was the charismatic newcomer who could effortlessly command a pulpit with passion and eloquence. Still, behind the preacher's collar, I was still a man grappling with the shards of his broken past.

One day, a call from a ghost of my past threatened to shatter the new life I had painstakingly built. The voice on the other end belonged to a friend with whom I had shared my transitional phase. The moment I answered, her voice bore an unfamiliar tone. There were a few elongated moments of silence, broken only by my repeated hellos. When she finally spoke, her words hit me like a sledgehammer, "You have a son."

My mind raced. How was this possible? Why had she kept this a secret for so long? Emotions swirled within me—shock, confusion, and a sense of betrayal. The gravity of the situation started to sink in, intensifying my feelings of guilt and embarrassment. The ideals I had upheld, especially the aspiration to avoid having a child outside of wedlock, seemed to have crumbled in an instant. The harsh repercussions of decisions made in pain were staring right back at me.

It was as if another choice I'd made, tainted by the fog of suffering, had come full circle. Now, I was confronted with the profound realization: I am a father. This new role came with a myriad of emotions and responsibilities. While I was trying to grapple with this identity, a deeper longing surfaced—my own yearning for a paternal figure.

The irony was inescapable. Here I was, stepping into the shoes of fatherhood, yet feeling like a lost child, seeking guidance and solace from a fatherly presence I never truly had. My stepdad made genuine efforts, and I always recognized that. We shared moments that I genuinely cherished, yet a subtle, internal void persisted that kept reminding me of the difference between biology and bond.

Even in our warmest interactions, a part of me felt the distinction – he wasn't my biological father. I appreciated his love for my mom; in fact, that was one thing that always resonated clearly. Yet, that didn't fill the paternal void I felt deep within.

It was my grandfather who had bridged that gap for me. To me, he wasn't just a grandparent. He was the paternal figure I gravitated towards, the guiding hand, the comforting presence. His wisdom, strength, and unconditional love provided the fatherly anchor I so desperately sought.

With him no longer by my side, that void felt even more profound. The absence of his guiding presence was a wound that time had yet to heal. This closeness of roles—being both a beacon of strength and security for my child while simultaneously seeking those very same pillars for myself—created a whirlwind of emotions. The journey of healing, understanding, and growth had taken yet another unexpected turn, challenging me to confront my past, embrace the present, and shape a future that would provide my son with everything I had yearned for.

The revelation of fatherhood ushered in a paradigm shift in my priorities and plans. I knew I had to be present in his life, even though the path forward was unfamiliar and intimidating. My heart was willing, even if my experience was lacking. I was determined to learn and evolve in this new role. Henceforth, every decision I made would need to factor in his well-being and future. The thought of relocation, too, loomed large, underscoring the profound changes that lay ahead.

I understood the significance of a father's role in a child's life cannot be overstated. Fathers are not just providers but pillars of strength, sources of wisdom, and role models for values and character. Research and countless anecdotes underscore the immense influence fathers have on their children's emotional and psychological well-being, academic achievements, and even their social behavior. A father's support can instill confidence, while his guidance can shape morals and ethics. In many ways, fathers help sculpt the lens through which children view the world.

Understanding this importance deepened my commitment. I was not just responsible for my son's material needs but for his emotional and psychological foundation as well. Even though the road ahead was uncertain, my resolve to be the best father remained. This revelation opened a Pandora's box of introspection. It confronted me with questions about responsibility, past decisions, and the path forward. Would I be able to reconcile with my past, embrace the unexpected present, and forge a future that aligned with my newfound faith and commitment? Only time would tell.

CHAPTER 6

FAITH'S FLOURISH

PAIN LEVEL 9

The Resilient Growth of Conviction

Though there's a glimmer of hope and connection, there's still a significant pain in rediscovering oneself. The decision was clear in my mind—I was moving back to Kentucky. It wasn't just about geographical proximity; it was about connecting with a part of myself I hadn't known existed—my son. It was an opportunity to play an active role in his life and to reestablish myself in familiar surroundings.

Life, with its challenges, reminded me that decisions have practical implications. Even with my military retirement, the funds weren't adequate to support the evolving demands of my new life. The job hunt began in earnest. Browsing through various listings, my eyes landed on a Juvenile Detention Center position. Given my background and experiences, it felt like a role I could truly step into.

However, as I embarked on this fresh start, my feelings were a whirlpool of hope and apprehension. Spirituality had been my anchor during the stormiest times, so finding a church in this new chapter of life was non-negotiable. I had evolved in my understanding of faith—it was no longer about ritualistic attendance but nurturing a deep, personal relationship with God. However, old scars and judgments can surface in the most unexpected places. Walking into the church with my son and his mother, I felt the weight of unsolicited glances and hushed murmurs.

Yet, in a twist of events, I found myself being called upon to make announcements in the church. They didn't know my past experiences or credentials; they just saw potential. As I spoke, I felt a surge of emotion and ended up sharing a personal testimony. The atmosphere in the church transformed. The energy, the joy, the Spirit—it was palpable. People were moved, and so was the pastor.

After the service, the pastor approached me, curiosity evident in the eyes. After inquiring about my past and speaking to my previous church, they presented an offer: would I consider leading the youth department? The proposal seemed divine. Working with the youth during the week and guiding them spiritually on weekends felt like a harmonious blend. Plus, it provided the perfect setting to introduce my son to the church community. Everything seemed to align seamlessly. Or so I thought.

The journey ahead was bound to unveil lessons, challenges, and growth in ways I couldn't yet fathom. Public speaking was a terrain I never imagined treading. The spotlight, gazes, and responsibility to articulate thoughts were all alien and intimidating. Yet, destiny, it seemed, had other plans. Time and again, life thrust me onto the dais, pushing me to face my fears.

When I was chosen as the graduation speaker for the Detention Center training program, a mix of trepidation and determination gripped me. Drawing from my faith, weaving in inspiration and motivation, I spoke from the heart. The applause, the standing ovation, it all seemed surreal. The Center Director's admiration was evident, and whispers of a promotion upon my return began to circulate. The accolades were overwhelming, and externally, it looked like everything was falling into place.

Beneath this veneer of success and acknowledgment lay a tumultuous storm. Behind the closed doors of my mind, battles raged on—some old, some new, but all equally debilitating. The world saw a man progressing, achieving, and leading. What they missed was the nightly hauntings, the memories that refused to fade, the demons that constantly clawed at my consciousness. With a smile that belied the anguish underneath, I reassured the world, saying, "I'm okay." But every day was a fight—against the past, the pain, and the ever-present specter of despair.

The increasing dosage of medication was a testament to the depth of this internal struggle, and on top of that, the weight of being a recognized man of faith amplified my inner turmoil. I had mastered the rhetoric, knowing precisely what to say and when, echoing the examples I'd seen. Yet, that crafted persona wasn't me at my core.

My upbringing championed brutal honesty—a trait that the military not only accepted but celebrated. However, the church, or at least my experience of it at that time, seemed less accepting of raw truths. I felt torn. On one hand, I was valued and appreciated for my ability to inspire and lead. On the other, I sensed that I was being utilized primarily for my gift of oration rather than being valued as a complete individual with complexities and vulnerabilities.

This tension between showcasing a polished facade and voicing my authentic feelings and struggles created a whirlpool of confusion. The juxtaposition of wanting to be genuine about my internal battles while meeting the expectations of the faith community became a challenging tightrope walk, each step fraught with internal conflict. Balancing fatherhood, confronting and mending my past wounds while maintaining the facade that all was well was an exhausting tightrope walk.

The church gave me a platform, a voice, and responsibilities. People saw the preacher, the confident voice guiding them toward faith and redemption. But very few glimpsed the man beneath the robe—the one scarred, haunted, and constantly seeking solace in a world that seemed both welcoming and hostile at the same time. The duality of my existence was both my strength and my most significant challenge.

My spiritual journey was blossoming in ways I had never anticipated. With the completion of my degrees in Theology and Interdisciplinary Studies, my understanding of faith and scripture deepened profoundly. The intricate art of exegetical study allowed me to unravel and appreciate the Bible in all its layers. But this rapid ascension in theological knowledge and the enthusiasm with which I approached ministry did not go unnoticed nor without judgment. A few veterans of the faith, who had spent decades within the church's walls, occasionally threw veiled jabs, hinting that I might be overstepping or "doing too much."

What they failed to grasp was that my relationship with God wasn't anchored in mere ritual or tradition—it was intensely personal. My passion stemmed from a profound connection, not from a need for recognition or to impress. As days turned into months and months into years, my commitment and sincerity did not go unnoticed by the church's leadership.

The pastor, who had now ascended to the esteemed position of a Bishop, saw in me a reflection of genuine dedication to the cause. The church leaders proposed that I be ordained as an elder. When this was discussed in a formal setting, I made it clear: my purpose wasn't to chase titles or accolades. For me, it was a mission to reach out, touch lives, and bring back those who felt alienated or lost.

I saw myself in every lost sheep, for there was a time when I, too, had wandered, seeking purpose and meaning. It was the relentless love of Jesus that had sought and found me. Now, it was my turn to be that beacon of hope for others.

Indeed, this powerful biblical imagery from the Parable of the Lost Sheep beautifully captures the essence of Jesus' teachings on love, redemption, and relentless pursuit. In the Gospel of Luke 15:3-7, Jesus tells the parable of a shepherd who leaves his ninety-nine sheep in the wilderness to seek out the one that is lost. Isn't it amazing how it shows that being in the wilderness is better than being lost?

When he finds it, he rejoices and calls his friends and neighbors to celebrate with him. The message is clear: every single soul is of immense value to God, and He rejoices over everyone's return to Him. This parable highlights the profound love and commitment of God towards His children, emphasizing that He cares deeply for every single individual, no matter how far they have strayed.

It's a reminder of God's boundless love and His desire for all to be saved, showing that no one is beyond redemption. This message is especially powerful for those who feel lost or distant from God, reassuring them that they are always loved and that there's always a way back into His embrace. It's this belief, rooted deeply within my heart and soul, that drove me.

While the concept resonated with many community leaders and drew admiration, it also met with skepticism from others. Perhaps it was my unconventional approach to ministry that raised eyebrows. I wasn't tethered to the pulpit or swayed by monetary incentives. Instead, I found my congregation in the most unexpected places—park benches, bustling Walmart parking lots, local corner stores, and even the "rough" neighborhoods.

To the young souls at the Juvenile Detention Center, I broke down scripture in a language they could relate to, showing them that redemption and hope weren't reserved for the 'perfect' or the 'righteous' but were accessible to all. If I could change the trajectory of even one life, I believed my mission would be successful. Yet, for all the spiritual battles I fought on the outside, my inner demons remained undefeated.

As the date of my ordination approached—a recognition of my dedication and commitment—my life seemed to spiral into chaos. Relationships that once seemed rock-solid began to crumble. Emotions, past regrets, and overwhelming responsibilities bombarded me, creating a whirlwind of despair. I felt out of sync with the world, grappling with a mounting sense of inadequacy. The haunting thought that I wasn't 'good enough' or 'I wasn't like them' consumed me. In these moments of overwhelming darkness, verses that once brought solace slipped away, and the fragmented pieces of my soul felt irreparable.

Two weeks before the day that was supposed to be a hallmark of my spiritual journey, I found myself sinking into a chasm of desolation. Sitting alone on my living room couch, the weight of life's trials and tribulations bore down on me, making the idea of surrender—the ultimate surrender a tempting escape. The world's noise faded, replaced by a deafening silence, as I contemplated the unthinkable. The path ahead seemed insurmountable, and in that bleak moment, I considered waving the final white flag.

The unexpected interruption of my thoughts by the persistent knocking was puzzling. Opening the door to find a church friend, with his radiant smile and warm demeanor, felt like a jarring contrast to the storm brewing inside me. As he entered, his words flowed, expressing appreciation and gratitude for all I had done. Yet, my mind, trapped in its spiral of darkness, barely registered what he was saying. His words felt like distant echoes, overshadowed by the overwhelming noise of my internal struggles.

Using the bathroom as an excuse, I momentarily distanced myself, hoping to gather my thoughts and regain some semblance of control. When I returned, I found the living room empty—my friend was gone. A part of me felt relieved, as his presence had only amplified my internal turmoil. Alone again, I settled back into my chair, the weight of despair settling over me.

With a loaded gun, my mind was set, the path clear. But as I acted on that dark impulse, God had a different plan. Click, and then, nothing. The silence that followed was deafening, thick with implications and unanswered questions. Being a weapons expert, I knew about guns, especially mine. I looked at it and noticed the clip was missing. The realization hit me with the force of a tidal wave. The missing clip was not an accident or oversight; my friend had intentionally taken it out.

Yet, as the layers of understanding settled, another realization struck even harder: even with a bullet still chambered, the weapon had refused to fire. Despite my mind being clouded by despair, I could see it clearly now—this was divine intervention. God had stepped in when I was at my lowest ebb.

A surge of mixed emotions overcame me. Gratitude for being given another chance, bewilderment at the sequence of events that had transpired, and an underlying sense of shame for having even considered such a final act. That night, my living room became both the scene of my deepest despair and the birthplace of my renewed hope.

The reality of the experience, the sheer weight of the divine intervention, was a testimony. But sharing it? That thought brought a fresh wave of apprehension. The church, the community, the world at large—they all saw one version of me. How could I reveal such a stark, raw, and vulnerable side of myself? This event, like so many others in my past, seemed destined to become another concealed scar, a secret chapter in the ongoing narrative of my life. It was also a poignant reminder that even in the darkest moments, there's a higher power watching over, guiding, and protecting.

That night, as the hours ticked by, the silence of my living room bore witness to a man grappling with his existence, his purpose, and the guiding hand of destiny. The room, which had almost become a place of eternal silence, now echoed with renewed promises and whispered prayers. The scars of my past and present may have been concealed, but they also served as silent reminders of resilience, battles fought and won, and the ever-present guiding hand of God even in the darkest times. As dawn broke, a new chapter awaited, filled with challenges and revelations that would test the very core of my being.

CHAPTER 7

FRACTURED FRIENDSHIPS

PAIN LEVEL 7

Life's intricacies don't pause, especially in the realm of relationships. While my internal battles raged, the external dynamics with friends and acquaintances added layers of complexity. It's one thing to struggle personally but entirely another to manage the perceptions, judgments, and expectations of those around you. In the military, there was a clear chain of command and structure. But here, in the community of faith, lines are often blurred, influenced heavily by emotions, faith, and perceptions.

I was at a crossroads, grappling with profound questions about my purpose and calling. The looming ordination felt more like a noose tightening around my neck than a collar symbolizing divine calling. With all the doubts clouding my mind, I felt the need to confide in someone, to share the burdens of my heart. I approached one of the senior church leaders, hoping for insight and guidance.

"Some of life's best lessons are learned at the worst times."-Unknown

Yet, the response I received was disheartening. Instead of the understanding and support I yearned for, I was met with the ever-familiar platitudes. "You're too anointed for this," he quipped, almost dismissively. "Just pray about it." While the power of prayer was undeniable, what I needed at that moment was human understanding and empathy, not just spiritual bypassing.

It was a realization that while I might stand on the pulpit, delivering sermons infused with hope and faith, there was a stark disconnect between the preacher and the man behind it. The weight of expectations, the pressure to always be 'on,' and the relentless demand to mask my vulnerabilities were taking a toll. The pulpit became something like my shield, protecting me from confronting the raw, unvarnished truths of my life. But shields, no matter how strong, eventually crack under pressure. I was nearing my breaking point, and something had to give.

The very friendships that were supposed to be the pillars of support sometimes felt like sand slipping through my fingers. Misunderstandings arose, loyalties were questioned, and the pain from these fractures often overshadowed my internal struggles. Whispers circulated, and confidential conversations that I believed were safely tucked away within the sacred walls of the church became fodder for idle chatter, spreading like wildfire. It was as if my life, with all its intricacies, had been turned into the latest episode of some reality show, discussed, and dissected for all to hear.

It wasn't just about disagreements or differences in opinions; it was the realization that even the most trusted allies could sometimes fail to understand the depth of one's pain. Do they forget that I am not infallible, not the savior they perhaps expect me to be? I'm a man, deeply scarred and carrying a multitude of internal wounds, wounds that I fervently wish would heal. Each day is a balance for me, swinging between moments of spiritual elation and profound despair.

I'm constantly on the verge. Just one prayer away from praise is what I do to utterly tear Da club up. I may be saved by grace, but I still bear the weight of my human frailty, constantly teetering on the edge. The sanctity of trust isn't merely a value; for someone grappling with PTSD, it's a lifeline.

Trust, in essence, forms the bedrock of any relationship, a silent agreement that the sanctuary of our shared truths will remain inviolable. When that trust is betrayed, it doesn't merely cause disappointment; it ravages the very core of our belief in people, especially when you're already dealing with the scars of PTSD. For someone with PTSD, trust is not just a matter of emotional security; it's about psychological safety. PTSD isn't just about reliving traumatic events; it's about navigating the world with a heightened sense of vulnerability, always on the defensive, always on edge.

In such a fragile state of mind, trust becomes more than just a feeling; it becomes a necessity, a buffer against a world that often feels hostile and unpredictable. Every breach of that trust feels like a personal affront, a betrayal that reopens old wounds and, in many cases, inflicts new ones. The heart of the issue isn't just about the act of divulging a secret or breaking a confidence; it's about the profound sense of isolation and abandonment it fosters.

For someone with PTSD, this feeling is magnified manifold, taking them back to those moments of trauma when they felt most alone, most vulnerable. When trust is broken, it feels like being pushed back into that abyss of despair, reinforcing the feeling of being perpetually unsafe and perpetually misunderstood. So, when I speak about trust, it isn't just a whim or a principle; it's a plea for understanding, for compassion. It's a request to be seen, heard, and most importantly, protected in one's moments of profound vulnerability. It's about preserving that thin line of hope that connects one to the world, that keeps the darkness of the past from engulfing the present.

Still, amidst this tumultuous landscape of relationships, some bonds grew stronger, forged in the crucible of shared pain and mutual understanding. These were the friendships that reminded me of the importance of genuine connection, of having someone to lean on when the weight of the world threatened to crush the spirit. As each day unfolded, the rifts in some relationships grew evident, demanding introspection, understanding, and sometimes the strength to let go. The journey ahead was not just about personal healing but also about understanding the dynamics of friendships and the pain that comes from their frictions.

> *"Sometimes we maintain relationships because we are afraid of the unknown, even when the known is more painful."*

Choosing from a place of pain, I discovered, often led to decisions clouded by emotions, unmet needs, and unresolved traumas. While pain might temporarily blur one's vision, the repercussions of those choices often have long-lasting effects, not just on oneself but also on others involved. It's a bitter truth I had to confront repeatedly. In my quest for solace, I often mistook transient pleasure for lasting happiness. But fleeting moments of ecstasy couldn't fill the gaping void within.

Pleasure, when sought as an escape, can often become a mirage, enticing and promising but disappearing upon closer inspection. The allure of momentary relief often overshadowed my deeper purpose, leading me down paths that seemed right but were mere detours from my true calling. Time and time again, I've gravitated towards relationships, hoping their presence would mend my fractured soul.

These relationships were chosen from a place of brokenness. I was trying to find myself in the reflections of others, hoping that they would piece together the shattered fragments of my identity. In doing so, I inadvertently inflicted pain on them. I dragged them into the maelstrom of my personal battles, making them casualties of my internal wars. Their time and emotions became the unintended price for my misguided choices.

Looking back, I recognize the trail of hurt I left behind. Relationships or marriages built on unstable foundations of pain and pretense are bound to crumble. Authenticity and truth have a way of shining through, no matter how much we try to obscure them. Like gold refined by fire, genuine connections and purpose can withstand the heat and pressure of life's trials. Anything counterfeit eventually reveals itself under such scrutiny.

"Growth is painful. Change is painful. But, nothing is as painful as staying stuck where you do not belong." - N. R. Narayana Murthy

It's a hard lesson but an invaluable one. To truly find ourselves and connect with others, we must first heal, ensuring that our choices align with our authentic selves and higher purpose rather than being mere reactions to our pain. Our lives are a tapestry woven from the threads of choices, experiences, and relationships. Some of these threads are vibrant, reflecting moments of joy, love, and connection. Others are darker, manifesting as deep-seated heartaches, regrets, and scars.

My journey, particularly through this chapter, has been one of introspection and realization of the intricate web of relationships that formed my personal tapestry. Each thread, no matter how painful or beautiful, has a purpose and a lesson. I've learned that your healing matters. I'll touch more on that later....

The very essence of 'Fractured Friendships' has been the discovery of these lessons. How our choices, particularly those stemming from a place of pain, reverberate through our relationships, altering their course, sometimes momentarily, and at other times, irrevocably. The fractures, the breaks, and the chasms that form due to these choices are painful but essential. It's within these fractures that we truly see ourselves, our vulnerabilities, and our strengths.

"Prioritizing self-care, perceiving it not as a luxury, but as essential, allows us to show up in the world as our best selves." -Dr. Shumonte Cooper

Like any good tapestry, the beauty isn't in the individual threads but in the overall design. A design that is always evolving and always in flux. The concept of healing the fractured and broken places in life draws a poignant parallel to the Japanese art of Kintsugi. Kintsugi, meaning "golden joinery," is a centuries-old practice of mending broken pottery with lacquer dusted or mixed with powdered gold, silver, or platinum. This philosophy treats breakage and repair as part of the history of an object rather than something to disguise or discard.

In the context of human experience, Kintsugi serves as a metaphor for embracing our imperfections and finding beauty in the healing process. Just as Kintsugi highlights the cracks in pottery with precious metals, we can learn to value the scars and fissures in our lives. These imperfections are not just reminders of what has been broken and lost but integral to our story, marking our resilience and capacity to recover.

Healing the broken places in life is about acknowledging and respecting our past hardships, not as mere flaws or weaknesses, but as essential parts of our unique identity. It teaches us that there is strength in vulnerability and beauty in the journey of repair. In this way, our healed wounds, much like the Kintsugi pottery, become symbols of hope and transformation, shining with the golden seams of our experiences.

The value of this healing lies in its ability to transform our perspective. It encourages us to shift our focus from what we have lost to what we have gained: wisdom, strength, compassion, and a deeper appreciation for the fragile yet precious nature of life. This shift in perspective can lead to a more fulfilled and authentic existence, where we honor all parts of our journey, both the broken and the healed.

Just as Kintsugi transforms broken pottery into a new work of art, the process of healing our broken places allows us to emerge as more complex, resilient, and beautiful individuals. It's a testament to the fact that it's not just about putting back the broken pieces but also about reinventing ourselves through the process of recovery, proudly bearing the golden seams of our experiences.

As this chapter comes to a close, I find solace in the knowledge that while there have been painful threads, there have also been threads of healing, understanding, and growth. These threads will guide my journey into a realm of recovery and rebuilding. As we transition from the tumultuous landscapes of fractured friendships and relationships, we embark on a new chapter and a new phase, one that holds the promise of healing and hope.

CHAPTER 8

FORTIFIED FRAMEWORK

PAIN LEVEL 4

The recovery brings relief, yet some days are better than others. I've come to understand that the path of healing isn't linear. It's a winding road with its peaks and valleys, moments of clarity contrasted with moments of doubt. With every step, the framework of my life, once fragile and brittle, starts to fortify.

The lessons from the past serve as the foundation for this new framework. With each layer, there's a strengthening, a resilience that emerges, not from the avoidance of pain but from acknowledging and understanding it. This fortified framework isn't about building walls or shutting out experiences; it's about having the strength and wisdom to face them head-on, to absorb, learn, and grow.

However, even in this phase of fortification, there are days when the weight of past choices and experiences bear down. Days when the shadows of 'Fractured Friendships' creep in, casting doubts and reviving old heartaches. Yet these moments, too, are part of the recovery. In these moments of vulnerability, I'm reminded of the importance of continuous growth and introspection.

"Although the world is full of suffering, it is also full of the overcoming of it." - Helen Keller

As this new chapter unfolds, the emphasis shifts from merely healing to truly understanding the strength that lies within, which has been honed and refined through the fires of trials and tribulations. The 'Fortified Framework' is more than just a shield; it's a testament to human resilience, to the ability to rebuild, stronger and wiser, no matter the adversities faced. In this journey of fortification, while pain still registers at level 4, there's an underlying current of hope, signaling that the best is yet to come.

"Your illness does not define you. Your strength and courage do."-Dr. Shumonte Cooper

My faith was my rock, my anchor, guiding me through the treacherous waters of pain and medication dependency. The medicine, for all its supposed benefits, felt like chains binding me, preventing me from truly living, from feeling, from connecting. While many rely on them to survive, to me, it felt like a prison. The allure of the quick fix, the immediate relief it promised, was tantalizing, but the price was too high. Each pill represented a moment I was not truly present, an emotion I did not truly feel, a part of me that remained detached from the world.

I remember nights spent staring at those tiny capsules, the weight of the decision pressing on me. Could I truly be free of them? The self-doubt would often creep in, but with every bottle I emptied into the toilet, a part of my hope was restored. It was symbolic, flushing away my dependency, my reliance on these substances that controlled so much of my life.

Of course, the journey wasn't easy. The physical symptoms, the withdrawal, and the ever-present migraines made some days unbearable. It was a battle with victories and defeats. Yet, with each passing day, I felt stronger, more connected to the world, and more in tune with my emotions.

I was often met with skepticism and doubt. Friends, family, and even strangers would offer their unsolicited advice. "Why would you put yourself through this?" They'd ask, not understanding that this pain was part of the healing and that I had to face it head-on to truly overcome it. They couldn't fathom why someone would willingly suffer when there was a "solution" at hand.

For me, true healing didn't come from a bottle. It came from within, my faith, and the determination to reclaim my life. The road ahead was still uncertain. But with every migraine-free day, with every symptom that slowly faded away, my conviction grew. I wasn't just aiming for relief; I was aiming for healing. I was aiming for a life unburdened by the shadows of the past, a life where pain was just a memory, not a daily reality.

It wasn't just the migraines that were a challenge, but the side effects of living in a constantly altered state. The window tint, though a minor adjustment, served as a daily reminder of my vulnerabilities. Every time I sat behind the wheel, I was reminded of the world I had to shield myself from. While others enjoyed the golden hues of a sunset or the luminescence of a full moon, these very beauties of nature became potential hazards for me.

Driving around, the tinted windows isolated me, turning my car into a dim sanctuary. Many alluded to it as a fashion statement, but it wasn't. While they shielded me from the painful glares, they also cast the world in a perpetual shade, dimming the vibrancy of life outside. There were days when I wished I could roll down the windows and let the sunlight wash over me to feel its warmth without the looming threat of a migraine.

Canceling plans became a dreaded routine. The disappointment in the voices of friends and family, the missed opportunities, the moments lost to searing pain - they all weighed heavy on my heart. There was a palpable tension every time I committed to an outing, and there was a lingering question: Would today be a good day? Or would the migraines strike again, leaving me incapacitated and missing out on another memory?

Through it all, I held on to hope. Every time I braced myself against the onslaught of pain, every time I chose to step out, even with the threat of a migraine looming, I was taking back control, one day at a time. It was a testament to my resilience, a quiet defiance against the circumstances. The journey was far from easy, but with every small victory, I was reminded of the strength within me, ready to face whatever came next.

Amidst the chaos of my internal struggles, Grandfather's voice in my head became the steadfast anchor, reminding me to persist, to endure, and to "Do the Work." His words resonated deeply, inspiring a resilience I didn't know I possessed. They fueled my determination to navigate through the unpredictable waves of physical and emotional pain.

The journey wasn't linear. As I said before, there were highs and devastating lows. Moments when progress felt tangible, and then faced with days when it seemed like I was back at square one. Navigating the labyrinth of triggers became an intricate dance. Something as innocuous as the scent of a particular dish or the hum of a certain tune could catapult me into a whirlwind of emotions or physical discomfort.

The weight of battling multiple disabilities was, at times, overwhelming. Every morning, as I woke up, it was as if I was rolling dice, unsure which combination of ailments would confront me. Yet, in the face of it all, there was a relentless desire, an innate drive, to reclaim the sense of self I felt had been taken from me. I wasn't just fighting for relief from the symptoms but for the reclaiming of my identity, my spirit, and my joy.

Clinical depression and anxiety, often silent tormentors, posed challenges of their own. They weren't as evident as a migraine or the visible hair loss, but their impact was profound. There were days filled with despair. Even the weight of my thoughts was crushing. Yet, every therapy session and every group meeting was a testament to my commitment. I wasn't just passively enduring but actively engaging in my recovery.

For over 15 long years, this became my rhythm—a dance of pain and healing, setbacks and breakthroughs. The journey was grueling, but every small victory was a glimmer of hope. I often found myself whispering silent prayers, yearning for a breakthrough, a respite from the seemingly endless cycle. Yet, with every challenge I faced and every day I survived, I was inching closer to the wholeness I so desperately sought.

As days turned into months and months into years, the framework of my life began to solidify. The work, though intense, had created a structure, a fortified framework, on which I could rebuild. With every bit of progress, a piece of me that had been lost to the abyss of pain and confusion was recovered. My narrative wasn't just about survival anymore; it was about thriving, about rediscovery.

"Out of suffering have emerged the strongest souls;
the most massive characters are seared with scars."
- Khalil Gibran

One evening, while reflecting on the journey, a realization washed over me. The very experiences that had threatened to shatter me had instead forged me into a stronger, more resilient individual. The crucible of my challenges had not just tempered my spirit but had given it a shine that was uniquely mine. My story wasn't defined by my pain but by the strength with which I faced it. With this newfound perspective, the chapter of "Fortified Framework" was ending, making way for a new dawn. As the sun set on the struggles of my past, a horizon of potential and promise began to emerge.

CHAPTER 9

TURNING THE CORNER

PAIN LEVEL 3

The metamorphosis was evident. The dark clouds of yesteryears were gradually giving way to clearer skies. My sense of self, once lost amidst the tumult of pain and chaos, was making its triumphant return. As it did, the grip of agony was slowly but surely loosening. The next phase wasn't just about navigating pain but embracing the potential of a future beautifully forged from the fires of my past. Moving forward wasn't merely about managing the anguish; it was about seizing the promise of a future crafted by overcoming the trials of my past.

Disaster preparation recovery and response have always been a fervent passion of mine. Deep down, I yearned to wholly embrace this calling, feeling it was interwoven with my destiny. However, my disabilities, particularly the debilitating migraines triggered by barometric pressure, often stood as formidable barriers. Yet, every time hurricanes battered the East Coast, I would muster all my strength and resources to assist those affected.

With each disaster, no matter how physically challenging it became, I rallied those willing to join me, and we set out to provide aid. It was bigger than me; I felt called to this. The essence of faith is not just belief but action—faith without works is dead. I yearned to be a vessel, to actively express my faith through service. In those moments, amidst the rubble and despair, I aimed to be the hands and feet of Jesus, bringing hope, relief, and solace to those in need.

Once, in the heart of a natural disaster in Wilmington, NC, amidst the chaos and devastation, I found myself fervently praying. I implored God to alleviate my suffering so I could wholly dedicate myself to this mission if it was truly my purpose. The constant physical pain was verging on insurmountable, yet an inner flame, an unyielding desire, fueled my persistence.

"Sometimes, the greatest test in life is being able to bless someone else while going through your own storm." -Dr. Shumonte Cooper

This path, I realized, wasn't about the destination but the journey itself. It was a journey filled with peaks and valleys, moments of doubt that threatened to overshadow moments of clarity. It was also marked by an unwavering spirit of persistence, hope, and faith. Even as the storms of migraines, anxiety, and depression loomed, I was convinced that they were temporary, that there existed a world where they couldn't touch me. My faith, however shaken at times, always guided me through the darkest hours, whispering that I was not alone.

About a year later, on a crisp Sunday morning in Atlanta, Georgia, I faced a defining moment. I visited a church to support a friend that would be ministering that day. The familiar throb of a migraine weighed heavily on me. Even as I sat in pain, I was reminded that God always has a plan, even when we can't see it. I felt a pull towards the altar. As I went to the front, a wave of vulnerability washed over me. It was a desperate plea for healing, a deep-rooted belief that today, God would intervene.

The hands that laid upon me were warm and comforting, and as I was prayed over, I believed. It was as if a heavy chain that had been coiled around my mind was unwinding. With every uttered word, every claim of faith, the weight was lifting. As I recount this narrative, chills still run down my spine.

In the vast sea of stories in the Bible, the tale of the crippled man waiting at Bethesda's pool for 38 years to be healed has always resonated deeply with me. I was 38 years old when I experienced my pivotal moment, on the brink of turning 39. My unwavering faith rested entirely in the Great Physician, believing wholeheartedly that miracles, like those of ancient times, still manifest in our lives today. It serves as a powerful metaphor for the lengths we go to, hoping for change but often finding ourselves bound by chains of our own making.

The crippled man's constant companion, the mat he lay upon, is emblematic. I see it as the M.A.T - "Multitude of Absent Things". It signifies the void many of us grapple with — the absence of God's healing in areas of our life that cripple our spirit, our aspirations, and our growth. It's a profound image of waiting — waiting for external circumstances to align, waiting for someone else to help us, waiting for a miracle. Yet, often, the miracle we await is within us.

At first glance, the question "Do you want to be made well?" appears to have a straightforward answer. Surely, one would think the response is an unequivocal 'yes.' However, as many of us have come to realize through the trials and tribulations of life, giving an answer is often the easiest part. The true challenge arises in the aftermath of our response.

As I steered my car towards home, a profound clarity began to wash over me. The relentless pounding that had gripped my head for what felt like an eternity was ebbing away. Each heartbeat seemed to distance me further from the agony that had become an unwelcome constant in my life. By the time I stepped over the threshold of my home, that debilitating migraine was nothing but a distant memory. It felt as if I had witnessed a miracle unfold right before my eyes. Deep within, an unshakeable conviction blossomed - I was touched and healed by God's grace.

Days seamlessly flowed into weeks, and weeks matured into months. The haunting pulse of a migraine, which once dictated the rhythm of my days, was nowhere to be found. This profound transformation served as a beacon of God's unwavering faithfulness. Every pain-free day from these was a testament to His infinite love and mercy. It was a poignant reminder that beyond the clutches of enduring pain lies a realm of healing and restoration. A realm that can

be accessed through fervent prayers, unyielding persistence, and an
unwavering flame of hope.

"The wound is the place where the light enters you." - Rumi

Chapter 10
Now What?
Pain Level 05

In January 2022, I confronted one of the most daunting experiences of my life. I was under the impression that I was having a heart attack. I went to urgent care, and they immediately sent me to the hospital. Lying in the hospital bed connected to an EKG machine, a tumult of emotions and reflections surged through me. Suddenly, the reality of mortality was staring back at me, and I felt utterly unready. So many dreams and aspirations still lingered unfulfilled. My year had begun on an exhausting note, and life's trials weren't done with me yet.

Later that year, I chanced upon a book written by a friend. In it, she detailed her journey battling and overcoming a type of skin cancer. Her story resonated with me, primarily because I noticed an eerily similar spot on my skin that seemed to be growing. Although months elapsed before I mustered the courage to have it examined, I couldn't ignore the changes. The spot had darkened, altered its form, and became itchy and irksome — sensations I hadn't felt before. When the diagnosis came back as Basal Cell Carcinoma, I was taken aback.

Old tendencies threatened to resurface. I considered concealing my scars and hiding from reality. Drawing inspiration from one of my friends, she encouraged me to face it. So, I decided to face my condition head-on, seeking treatment and eventual healing. Her strength gave me the push I needed to confront and conquer my fears. In those early days after the diagnosis, I grappled with a mix of emotions. There was the initial shock, of course, followed by bouts of denial, fear, and even embarrassment for some reason.

Why had I ignored the signs for so long? Why did I let my previous experiences cast a shadow on my ability to address this issue head-on? During my treatment, I learned that Basal Cell Carcinoma, if detected early, is highly treatable. But I also learned about its potential to be disfiguring and its capacity to spread if left untreated.

The road to recovery was a blend of medical treatments, emotional healing, and finding strength in the support of those whom I trusted. Sadly, there were only a few, but they were powerful! The scar that remained after the treatment was not just a mark on my skin but a symbol of the battles I had overcome – both physical and emotional.

Every glance at it reminded me of the fragility of life and the importance of proactive health management. Rather than hide this scar, I chose to wear it as a badge of courage, resilience, and triumph. However, through all of this, what stood out the most was the profound importance of awareness and early detection. If I had been more vigilant and knowledgeable about skin health, perhaps I could have detected and addressed it sooner. This realization reinforced the need for continuous self-awareness, especially when it comes to health.

This ordeal taught me the significance of listening to one's body, seeking timely medical advice, and leaning on true friends and family for support. It also underscored the value of sharing one's experiences to educate and help others. Amid this crisis, I grappled with the weight of depression, the confusion of a mid-life crisis, along with the private battle with skin cancer.

My journey through this phase was punctuated with numerous counseling sessions, interventions, and treatments. There was a period where I felt trapped in vulnerability, choosing to keep my struggles to myself. However, when I tried to open up to those I trusted with my private thoughts and frustrations, fragments of my personal life unintentionally came to light, even though all I yearned for was empathy and direction.

Then arrived the judgments, misconceptions, and further cracks in what was already a shaky foundation. In response, I morphed into a persona built out of sheer necessity for survival: a more reticent, impatient, curt, and distant version of myself. I lingered in this state for months, believing it was the refuge I required for preservation. The experience taught me the intricacies of vulnerability and the nuances of sharing one's pain.

Navigating through all these personal trials was further complicated as I pursued a Ph.D. and dealt with the reorganization of a nonprofit. Tack on the everyday challenges life throws at you, and it felt like an uphill battle. However, during those tumultuous times, I had a handful of steadfast individuals by my side. These friends were my beacon, providing consistent encouragement, timely correction, and sincere prayers. I will forever be indebted to and grateful for these unwavering few who stood by me.

Come 2023, I received the news that felt like a dawn after a long, dark night: I was cancer-free! No heart complications, and I was presented with a clean bill of health. As if to put a cherry on top of this newfound positivity, I walked across the graduation stage that June, marking not just an academic achievement but also a personal victory. Call me DR. Cooper!!!

When we speak of healing, it's easy to gravitate toward the physical bandages on wounds, casts on broken bones, and medicine for our ailments. However, a significant part of the healing process, often overlooked, is internal, invisible, and deeply personal. It is about belief, willpower, and an unyielding spirit. At the core of our internal healing process is belief.

When we believe in our capacity to heal, we become active participants in the process. This isn't about denying the existence or severity of an ailment but about fostering a mindset of resilience and hope. While the healing process begins from within, external support can amplify our internal efforts. Being surrounded by the right ones, or even being part of a support group, can provide emotional nourishment and strength.

I may look like what I been through, but it's a testament it didn't win! - Dr. Shumonte Cooper

To those still grappling with their storms, I am living proof that with faith and perseverance, you can emerge on the other side, whole, healed, and renewed. God is indeed faithful and a healer. The other side of pain is not just a destination; it's a testimony.

Chapter 11

Pain's Last Page, Hope's New Chapter

Pain Level 0

I reached a point of complete relief. The sensation of living without pain had become a distant memory, as it had been years since I experienced a day with a pain level of less than one. Yet, I persevered, committed not only to the healing process but also to holding onto the faith that my recovery would surpass my past state. Restoration is defined as the process of returning something to its original condition or ensuring its preservation. I've been blessed with more than just restoration — I've found forgiveness and redemption.

Today, I stand as a testament to personal resilience and a beacon of success. I am a published author. My words now serve as solace and inspiration to countless souls across the globe. Every chapter I've penned and every anecdote I've shared echoes the journey from darkness into light, mirroring the path I've walked.

With passion and determination driving me, I became a certified instructor for emergency management. Drawing from my own experiences and the strength I found within, I now guide others in preparing for, responding to, and recovering from disasters. I've always believed in equipping individuals with the necessary knowledge and skills, emphasizing that readiness can mean the difference between despair and hope.

Over the years, my mission has transcended its initial borders. What began as a personal journey soon expanded into a broader horizon, marked by a deep commitment to those in dire straits. As a response to my purpose with Christ is Relief, a 501c(3) organization, I've channeled my own pain and trials into a purpose that uplifts, empowers, and supports countless lives.

My endeavors did not stop there. Recognizing the silent heroes among us, I initiated 'Difference Makers™.' This platform isn't merely an accolade but a testament to the indomitable spirits that truly impact communities. These are the individuals who, through their resilience, empathy, and action, etch imprints of hope and positivity in the lives they touch.

On a more personal note, I ventured into the world of business with 'Cooper Enterprise.' More than just a commercial pursuit, it's a legacy project. I envisioned it as a sturdy bridge to the future, designed to ensure that my descendants, especially my children and their offspring, have a solid foundation and a promising tomorrow.

Parallel to my entrepreneurial and philanthropic journeys, I've been blessed with opportunities to be a voice of inspiration and hope. I've become a sought-after speaker, resonating messages of resilience, faith, and the profound wisdom of the gospel. Through my words, I strive to inspire, challenge, and ignite a flame of hope in every heart, reaffirming that no matter the magnitude of the storm, the human spirit can and will always rise above.

Over time, the impact of my endeavors has not gone unnoticed. The Governor of Kentucky graciously recognized my contributions and bestowed upon me the esteemed Kentucky Colonel Recognition in 2012. In 2022, I was profoundly humbled to receive the 'Humanitarian of the Year' award from Blacks in Nonprofits. The momentum continued into 2023 when I was conferred with the distinguished Global Humanitarian Award. Yet, the zenith of these acknowledgments was reached when the President of the United States expressed deep appreciation for my work by honoring me with the Presidential Lifetime Achievement Award.

These accolades, though deeply humbling, are not what drives me. Instead, they serve as affirmations that my journey — from the depths of pain to the pinnacle of purpose — resonates, inspires, and makes a tangible difference. Reflecting on this, I am reminded that life is not just about the battles we face but how we choose to confront them. I didn't allow pain to become a brick wall, halting my progress. Instead, I used it as a stepping stone, pushing through every barrier, every challenge, every shadow of doubt. I transformed pain into power, darkness into dawn.

In life, we all navigate through storms, some more turbulent than others. Yet, it is essential to internalize this truth: you are not defined by the damage you've endured but by the strength you discover within yourself amidst adversity. Our experiences, no matter how painful, carve out spaces within us - not of emptiness, but of profound depth and capacity for resilience.

To everyone grappling with challenges, understand this: your present circumstances are merely a chapter, not the entirety of your story. The adversities you face today are but stepping stones. They are indelible marks of your bravery. They signify battles faced, lessons learned, and the myriad of times you refused to be broken. Wear them as medals of honor, showcasing your enduring spirit and the mountains you've conquered.

It is so easy in our moments of pain to feel isolated, to believe that we are alone in our suffering. Remember, every individual you admire, every hero you've looked up to, has faced their share of battles. It's not the absence of struggles that defines greatness but the ability to rise every time we fall. "For though the righteous fall seven times, they rise again."

In this vast expanse of life, filled with highs and lows, there lies a world brimming with opportunities and new beginnings. Behind every shadow of doubt, a realm of boundless possibilities is waiting to be unlocked. Your journey might be paved with challenges, but it's also adorned with dreams waiting to be realized.

So, when the weight of the world seems unbearable and when darkness seems unending, hold onto hope. Remember, the night is darkest just before the dawn. Your dawn is coming. Embrace it with open arms and an open heart, for even in your damage, you are far from being done. Welcome to the Other Side of Pain

> *"Being whole doesn't mean being more than who you are, at this moment — it means being who you are, at this moment." - Rachel Naomi Remen*

Chapter 12

As we reach the conclusion of our journey through "The Other Side of Pain," I want to leave you with a message of unwavering hope and encouragement. This final chapter is not just an ending but a beginning—the dawn of a new day, a time for renewal and growth. Throughout this book, we've explored the dark valleys of pain and the battles we face, both internally and externally. I understand the depth of the struggle. But here, in this concluding chapter, I invite you to step into the light of hope.

Hope is the North Star in our darkest night. It guides us when we are lost and strengthens us when we are weak. Remember, healing is not a destination but a journey. It's okay to not be okay, to have days where the pain seems insurmountable. Yet, it's crucial to hold onto hope, for it is the promise of better days.

Encouragement comes from within and from those around us. Surround yourself with people who uplift you and see your strength even when you don't. Let their words and presence be a source of comfort and motivation. You are not alone in this fight. The human spirit is incredibly resilient; you are a testament to that resilience.

Take small steps forward. Healing is not about grand gestures. Healing is about the small, consistent steps you take every day. Each step, no matter how small, is a victory. Celebrate these victories. Embrace the progress, however slow it might seem.

Be kind to yourself. You have been through a battle, and you are still standing. That in itself is remarkable. Treat yourself with the same compassion and understanding you would offer someone else.

Finally, look forward to new beginnings. The journey of healing opens new doors, teaches us new lessons, and brings new opportunities. It shapes us into stronger, more empathetic individuals. Embrace the changes, for they are part of your growth.

In the complex journey of life, marked by trials and tribulations, the power to win even while wounded is a profound testament to the resilience of the human spirit. This resilience is often fortified by faith and belief. This strength is not just about overcoming physical adversities. It delves deeper into the resilience of a soul that faces and overcomes adversity through faith and personal testimony.

Physical, emotional, or psychological wounds are not merely obstacles but catalysts for inner growth and strength. This strength emerges not despite our wounds but because of them, often guided by the belief in the redemptive power of the blood of the Lamb and the transformative nature of our testimonies.

I'm a living testament of this verse: "But He was wounded for our transgressions, He was bruised for our iniquities; The chastisement for our peace was upon Him, and by His stripes, I am healed." This verse from Isaiah 53:5 speaks profoundly to my Christian faith, reminding me that Jesus Christ's suffering and sacrifice were not in vain but for the ultimate redemption and healing of humanity, including myself.

This foundational belief reinforces the importance of not losing hope, even when circumstances around me seem utterly hopeless. It resonates with the principle in Hebrews 11:1, "Now faith is the substance of things hoped for, the evidence of things not seen." I've learned that faith is not merely a belief but a confident assurance in what I hope for, even without physical evidence.

In my moments of struggle and despair, these verses serve as a vital reminder to never let go of hope. The wounds and sacrifices mentioned in Isaiah symbolize the ultimate source of hope and healing available to me as a believer. This hope is not just a fleeting emotion but a steadfast anchor deeply rooted in my faith. When I was faced with challenges that seemed insurmountable, these scriptures encouraged me to cling to my faith, understanding that it is the very foundation of my hopes.

The interplay of these verses underscores a fundamental truth in my journey: through my belief in the sacrifices made for me and by holding onto hope and faith, even in the darkest of times, I find strength and healing. It's a powerful message that inspired me to maintain my hope and faith, drawing strength from the spiritual truths that underpin my beliefs. This tenet serves as a source of comfort and empowerment, encouraging me to face life's challenges with resilience and confidence, secure in the knowledge that faith and hope were the bedrock of my healing journey.

It is in the act of confronting and sharing our vulnerabilities and scars that we find our true power—a power that is deeply intertwined with our faith and personal stories. This power is about more than overcoming; it's about using our struggles as sources of strength, allowing us to rise not merely as survivors but as victors who have triumphed through faith. The journey through hardship, each wound, and challenge becomes a powerful testament to faith and perseverance, reminding us that our greatest victories often come from our most arduous battles.

As we face more challenges and celebrate more triumphs, we are encouraged to keep hope as our steadfast companion. In the words of the renowned poet Maya Angelou, "We may encounter many defeats, but we must not be defeated." Let this be your mantra. Stand tall, face the sun, and step forward into the dawn of renewal.

About the Author

Dr. Shumonte Cooper, a service-disabled army veteran, has transitioned his unwavering commitment from the battlefield to the forefront of humanitarian aid and disaster relief. As the CEO and founder of Christ is Relief Inc., his over two decades of dedication have been marked by significant achievements and recognition, including the Kentucky Colonel for humanitarian efforts, the 2022 Humanitarian of the Year award, and the prestigious Presidential Lifetime Achievement Award in 2023. His military discipline and strategic acumen have been pivotal in his approach to disaster response, embodying resilience, leadership, and compassion.

Educated at Harvard University, Liberty University, and Texas A&M Engineering, Dr. Cooper has specialized in Disaster Recovery and Terrorism Awareness Emergency Response, equipping him with unparalleled expertise in navigating crises. His certifications, including OSHA, CERT, and others, further attest to his comprehensive understanding of emergency response.

Dr. Cooper leverages his military experience and humanitarian passion to alleviate suffering and rebuild communities.

His efforts provide immediate relief and foster long-term resilience and recovery. This biography captures the essence of a man devoted to serving others, making a profound difference through his leadership, expertise, and unwavering dedication to humanitarianism.

Made in the USA
Columbia, SC
10 January 2025

50550602R00067